best recipes for absolutely everything

best recipes for

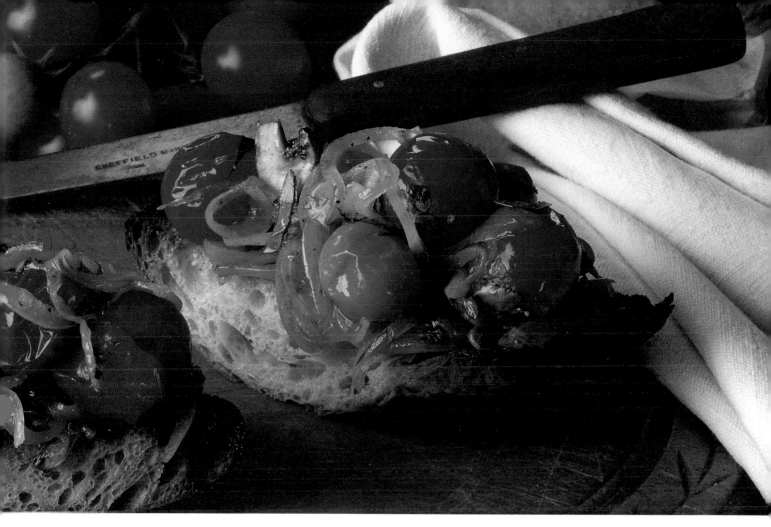

absolutely everything
ANNE WILLAN

ALHAMBRA
EDITIONS

This edition first published in 2005 by
Alhambra Editions,
Alhambra House,
27-31 Charing Cross Road,
London WC2H OLS

Based on material originally published in
Cooked to Perfection

Editorial Director: Jane O'Shea
Creative Director: Helen Lewis
Editor & Project Manager: Lewis Esson
Design: Paul Welti
Design Production Service: Keith Holmes,
Redbus
Production: Rebecca Short

Cataloguing in Publication Data: a catalogue
record for this book is available from the
British Library

ISBN 1 84400 252 7

Printed and bound in China

Contents

Introduction

This collection of recipes came about in a very particular way, as each recipe was originally specially selected or created to accompany and illustrate text and photographs that showed the reader how to cook every type of ingredient just right (now published in this book's companion volume, *How to Cook Absolutely Everything*). As a result, we suddenly discovered that we had a rather unusual compilation of dishes that covered a much wider range of main ingredients than most.

What's more, we had carefully chosen each recipe to make the most of that ingredient, producing, in effect, a showcase of the best recipes for absolutely everything... well almost everything! I hope at the very least that you can always find in this book a recipe for whatever you want to cook, and it will be one you will come back to again and again.

ANNE WILLAN

Fish & shellfish

Thank goodness for fish fillets. They can be cooked by almost any method and marry happily with a wide range of accompaniments, such as mushrooms, tomato, or other seafood such as prawns. I've always loved fillets of sole Florentine, in cheese sauce on a bed of spinach.

A cooked large whole fish is a joy to behold, especially when it is colourful like salmon and red snapper. a whole fish is ideal for barbecuing or try roasting it, Russian style, in sour cream.

Lobster salad is my first choice for enjoying the sweet flavour of this king of the sea, perhaps with pasta and asparagus, and classic lobster Newburg, served hot in a cream and Cognac sauce, remains hard to beat.

The meat inside steamed or boiled crab should be

wonderfully spicy, an invitation to dipping in melted
butter, or adventurous combinations such as Spanish
centollos with tomato sauce, sherry and brandy.

Shrimp and prawns can be marinated in olive oil or
vodka and grilled, peeled or unpeeled, or boiled in dill
court-bouillon. In Brazil, prawns are cooked in coconut
milk with okra, celery and peppercorns.

In America you'll find baked clams Casino and
oysters baked *à la Rockefeller* with spinach and cheese
sauce. A Southern sandwich of stewed oysters in cream
sauce in a baguette makes a memorable treat.

Belgians load outsized mussels with toppings of
onion, tomato and cheese. Most often we cook mussels
à la marinière, with onion, white wine and parsley.

John Dory with roasted garlic butter sauce

John Dory is excellent pan-fried as in this recipe, but if you prefer a lighter dish, grill the fish instead. Plaice or sole fillets work equally well treated this way.

SERVES 4

**4 John Dory fillets
(about 750 g/1½ pounds),
without skin**

**45 g/1½ oz flour, seasoned with
salt and pepper**

**1 large tomato, peeled, seeded
and chopped**

1 tablespoon chopped basil

45 g/1½ oz butter

FOR THE ROASTED GARLIC
BUTTER SAUCE

1 whole head of garlic

1 tablespoon olive oil

**140 g/4½ oz butter, chilled and
cut into small pieces**

3 shallots, finely chopped

75 ml/2½ fl oz white wine

**75 ml/2½ fl oz dry white
vermouth**

1 tablespoon double cream

2 egg yolks

1 tablespoon chopped basil

salt and white pepper

First roast the garlic for the sauce. Preheat the oven to 175°C/350°F/gas4. Cut the top off the stem end of the garlic head to expose the cloves. Put in a small heatproof dish, brush with olive oil, cover with foil and roast until soft, 35-45 minutes. When the garlic is soft, squeeze the head and, with tip of a knife, pull each clove out of its skin. Chop the cloves.

Melt 15 g/½ oz of the butter in a saucepan, add the shallots and sweat until soft but not coloured, stirring occasionally, 2-3 minutes.

Add the garlic, wine and vermouth. Boil, stirring, until reduced to 3-4 tablespoons, almost to a glaze. Stir in the cream and boil for 30-60 seconds. Turn the heat to low and gradually whisk in the butter pieces to make a creamy sauce. Work on and off the heat, so the butter softens and thickens the sauce without melting to oil. Season with salt and white pepper and set aside.

Rinse the fillets and pat dry with paper towels. Coat with seasoned flour, patting to remove excess. Combine the tomato and basil in a small bowl and season to taste.

In a heavy frying pan, heat the butter until foaming and add the fillets, skinned side up. Fry over brisk heat until golden brown, 2-3 minutes. Turn over and brown the other sides, until the fish is done to your taste, 3-5 minutes. Transfer the fish to 4 heatproof plates.

Finish the sauce: in a medium saucepan, whisk the egg yolks with 2 tablespoons water over low heat until foamy and very thick, being careful not to 'scramble' the yolks, 1-2 minutes. Take from the heat and gradually whisk in the warm butter sauce. Stir in the basil and taste for seasoning.

Heat grill. Sprinkle chopped tomato and basil over fish, then coat with garlic sauce. Grill until the sauce is just browned, 3-5 minutes. Serve at once.

Grilled swordfish with roasted corn and tomato salsa

**Roasting raw kernels of corn in a heavy pan gives them a wonderful
smoky flavour – the perfect foil for meaty swordfish.**

SERVES 4

**4 swordfish steaks
(about 750 g/1 ½ pounds),
cut 2 cm/¾ inch thick**
2 tablespoons olive oil
salt and pepper

FOR THE ROASTED CORN AND
TOMATO SALSA

4 corn ears, husks removed
2 red peppers
2 tablespoons olive oil
1 onion, diced
**2 tomatoes, peeled, seeded and
coarsely chopped**
**75 g/2½ oz sun-dried tomatoes
in oil, coarsely chopped, plus
1 teaspoon of their oil**
**1 tablespoon sherry or red
wine vinegar**
**3-4 tablespoons chopped
coriander
juice of 1 lime**

First make the salsa. Preheat the grill. While it is heating, prepare the corn. Holding each ear upright, cut off the kernels with a sharp knife. Heat a large heavy-based frying pan without any fat over a high heat until almost smoking. Add the kernels and dry-roast until tender, smoky and dark, tossing continuously as they tend to stick, 4-5 minutes. Cook the peppers under the grill, turning them until the skin chars and bursts, 7-10 minutes. Put them in a plastic bag and leave to sweat and cool so the skins loosen. Peel the peppers, discarding cores and seeds. Dice the flesh.

Heat 1 tablespoon of the olive oil in a large frying pan. Add the onion and sauté until soft but not brown, 3-4 minutes. Off the heat, stir in the corn, tomatoes, sun-dried tomatoes, peppers, vinegar and remaining oil. Heat, stirring, until hot. Take from the heat and keep warm.

Rinse the fish steaks and pat dry. Brush with half the oil, season and set on oiled grill rack about 7.5 cm/3 inches from the heat. Grill for 3-4 minutes. Turn the steaks over, brush with the remaining oil and grill until done to taste, 2-3 minutes longer.

Meanwhile, stir the coriander and lime juice into the salsa, taste and adjust the seasoning. Make a bed of salsa on 4 warmed plates and place a swordfish steak on top of each. Serve at once.

Black-and-white stir-fried bream

The black of dried mushrooms contrasts with white strips of bream in this lively stir-fry. For best flavour, use Chinese black mushrooms or black chanterelles; tree ears will add colour and chewy texture but little taste.

SERVES 4

30 g/1 oz dried black mushrooms

500 g/1 pound bream fillets, free of skin and bones

3 tablespoons vegetable oil

1.25-cm/½-inch piece of ginger, finely chopped

2 garlic cloves, finely chopped

2 dried red chillies

2 spring onions, sliced

500 g/1 pound pak choy or chard, stems and green leaves shredded

125 ml/4 fl oz fish or chicken stock

2 tablespoons soy sauce

1 tablespoon rice wine

1 tablespoon cornflour, mixed to a paste with 2 tablespoons water

FOR THE MARINADE

1 tablespoon rice wine or dry sherry

½ teaspoon salt

¼ teaspoon shrimp paste

¼ teaspoon pepper

1 egg white, whisked until frothy

1½ tablespoons cornflour

1 tablespoon oil

First soak the mushrooms: put the dried mushrooms in a bowl and pour over boiling water to cover generously. Leave them to soak for 20-30 minutes, then drain and dry them on paper towels. Trim any tough stems and cut the mushrooms into 5-cm/2-inch pieces.

Meanwhile, marinate the fish: wash the fillets, dry on paper towels and cut them into 5-cm/2-inch strips. Put the strips in a bowl with the rice wine, salt, shrimp paste and pepper. Mix well, then add egg white, cornflour and oil, and stir until smoothly coated. Cover and chill for 15-30 minutes.

When ready to cook, heat the wok over high heat until very hot. Pour in oil to coat the base and sides, reserving 1 tablespoon. Heat over high heat for 30 seconds. Add the ginger, garlic and red chilli peppers and stir-fry until fragrant, about 30 seconds. Add the fish and spring onions and stir-fry rapidly 2-3 minutes until the fish turns white. Discard the chillies, transfer the fish mixture to a bowl and set aside.

Wipe the wok with paper towels and heat again until very hot. Add the remaining oil and heat for 15 seconds. Add the shredded pak choy and mushrooms and stir-fry over high heat until the stems of the pak choy are crisp-tender and the mushrooms are hot, 2-3 minutes. Stir in the stock, soy sauce and rice wine, mixing thoroughly.

Return the fish mixture to the wok and stir well. Add the cornflour paste and continue stirring over high heat until the sauce thickens, 1-2 minutes. Remove the wok from the heat, taste and adjust the seasoning with soy sauce.

Serve the stir-fry immediately.

Roasted red snapper with curried vegetables

An impressive whole red snapper is presented on a bed of roasted, spiced root vegetables. So the stomach cavity of the fish does not collapse during cooking, I suggest stuffing it with a bunch of celery tops or parsley. The garlic and shallots in the garnish retain most flavour if their skins are left on, so leave peeling to your guests.

SERVES 4-6

1 whole red snapper (about 1.8 kg/4 pounds), cleaned, scaled and trimmed
1 bunch of celery tops or parsley
1 lemon, sliced and the slices halved
about 2 tablespoons vegetable oil

FOR THE CURRIED VEGETABLES

125 ml/4 fl oz vegetable oil
500 g/1 pound carrots, peeled and quartered lengthwise
500 g/1 pound turnips, peeled and quartered
250 g/$\frac{1}{2}$ pound celeriac, peeled and cut into wedges
500 g/1 pound potatoes, peeled and quartered
8 shallots, unpeeled
8 garlic cloves, unpeeled
1 tablespoon curry powder
2 teaspoons sugar
75 g/2$\frac{1}{2}$ oz whole blanched almonds
1 teaspoon salt
1/2 teaspoon pepper

22.5x32.5-cm/9x13-inch flameproof roasting pan

Preheat the oven to 190°C/375°F/gas5. First prepare the curried vegetables: heat the oil in the roasting pan, add the carrots and sauté for 2 minutes. Stir in the turnips and celeriac and sauté for 2 minutes longer. Stir in the potatoes, shallots and garlic and sauté for 2 minutes more.

Mix the curry powder, sugar, almonds, salt and pepper in a small bowl. Sprinkle over the vegetables and toss with two spoons until well mixed. Transfer to the preheated oven and roast the vegetables, stirring occasionally, for 25-30 minutes, until starting to soften and brown.

Meanwhile, rinse the snapper skin and cavity, and pat dry with paper towels. Stuff the bunch of celery tops or parsley in the cavity of the fish. Diagonally slash one side of the fish 3-4 times and insert one or two half lemon slices in each slash.

After the vegetables have roasted for 25-30 minutes, set the fish on top of them. Brush with oil and sprinkle with salt and pepper. Return the pan to oven and roast until fish is done and vegetables are tender and browned, 30-35 minutes. During cooking, baste the fish often with the cooking juices. If the fish is done before the vegetables, transfer it to a warmed platter and keep warm while the vegetables finish cooking.

Carefully lift the fish from the roasting pan and transfer to a warmed platter. Spoon the vegetables and almonds around the snapper and baste it with the cooking juices. Carve it at the table.

Fish escalopes with mustard and tarragon

This quick little supper dish uses thin slices of fish cut at an angle from a whole fillet. Large firm fillets from any suitably sized fish can be used, including sea bass, halibut and salmon. A bowl of spinach noodles makes a delicious accompaniment for the cream sauce.

SERVES 4-6

1 large fish fillet (about 750 g/1½ pounds), with the skin
1 carrot, cut into julienne strips
green part of 1 leek, cut into julienne strips
salt and pepper
15 g/½ oz butter
250 ml/8 fluid ounces double cream
2 teaspoons Dijon mustard, or to taste
2 tablespoons chopped fresh tarragon, plus 4-6 whole sprigs for decoration

large non-stick frying pan

To make the escalopes: using a long sharp knife, cut the fish fillet at an angle into the largest possible slices about 6 mm/¼ inch thick, working towards the tail and discarding the skin.

To cook the julienned vegetables: bring a pan of salted water to the boil, add the carrot and leek, and boil until just tender but still firm, 3-5 minutes. Drain, rinse with cold water and drain again thoroughly. The fish and vegetables can be refrigerated for up to 4 hours.

To finish the dish: sprinkle the escalopes with salt and pepper. Heat the frying pan until hot, then brush it with the butter. Add as many escalopes as will fit in a single layer and cook until lightly browned, about 1 minute. Turn them and brown the other sides. Remove them from the pan and keep them hot while cooking the rest.

Add the cream to the pan and bring it to the boil. Whisk in the mustard, salt and pepper and add the vegetable julienne. Heat gently for 1 minute, then stir in the tarragon. Taste the sauce and adjust the seasoning.

Arrange the escalopes on warmed individual plates, allowing 2-3 per person. Spoon over the sauce partly to cover them, top with a tarragon sprig and serve.

Omelette Arnold Bennett

Arnold Bennett was a famous Victorian writer and critic who stayed for some time at London's celebrated Savoy Hotel while writing his novel *Imperial Palace*, based on life in a grand hotel. The Savoy's chefs created this dish for him, which he loved so much he had it made for him wherever he went in the world thereafter, and the dish is still a feature of the Savoy Grill's menu. It consists quite simply of an omelette flavoured with smoked haddock, then topped with cream and grated cheese before being browned under the grill. It makes a delectable brunch dish and any cooked smoked fish can be substituted for the haddock – smoked salmon is a particular treat.

SERVES 2

1 medium fillet of undyed smoked
   haddock (about 375 g/³⁄₄ pound)
375 ml/12 fluid ounces milk
6 eggs
salt and pepper
30 g/1 oz butter
3-4 tablespoons double cream
3-4 tablespoons grated Gruyère cheese

25-cm/10-inch omelette pan

Put the haddock in a frying pan, pour over the milk and cover with foil or a lid. Bring to a simmer and cook the haddock gently until it flakes readily, 8-10 minutes. Let it cool to tepid in the milk.

Drain the fish and flake the meat with your fingers, discarding skin and bones. Whisk the eggs with salt and pepper just until frothy. Preheat a hot grill.

Heat the butter in the omelette pan until it stops foaming. Immediately add the eggs and cook them over high heat, stirring briskly with a fork. After about 30 seconds, when the eggs are lightly thickened, stir in the flaked haddock. Continue stirring until the omelette is firm but still soft on top, 45-60 seconds.

Take the omelette from the heat, spoon over the cream and sprinkle with cheese. Grill it until lightly browned, 1-2 minutes. Slide it onto a hot dish and serve at once.

Salmon and scallop terrine with ginger sauce

Delicate scallop mousseline, striped with pink-fleshed salmon fillets, is equally good served hot with this tangy fresh ginger sauce or chilled with either a piquant mayonnaise or a walnut oil vinaigrette. Accompany with melba or wholemeal toast.

SERVES 6-8

250 g/½ pound salmon fillet, without
   skin, cut into strips
½ each green and red peppers,
   cored, seeded and chopped
2 canned truffles, with their liquid
   (optional)
bunch of watercress (optional)

FOR THE SCALLOP MOUSSELINE

750 g/1½ pounds sea scallops
3 egg whites
pinch of grated nutmeg
salt and white pepper
250 ml/8 fl oz double cream

FOR THE GINGER SAUCE

375 g/12 oz butter, cold and cut into
   pieces
2 garlic cloves, crushed
1 small onion, sliced
1 shallot, sliced
bouquet garni
5-cm/2-inch piece of fresh ginger,
   chopped
125 ml/4 fl oz white wine

1.25-litre/2-pint terrine mould or loaf
   pan

Preheat the oven to 175°C/350°F/gas4 and butter the mould or pan. Bring a small pan of salted water to the boil, add the peppers and boil for 1 minute to blanch. Drain, rinse in cold running water and drain thoroughly. Drain the truffles, if using, reserving liquid; chop one and slice the other.

Make the scallop mousseline: whisk the egg whites until foamy. In a food processor, work the scallops to a fine purée. With the blades still turning, gradually work in the egg whites. Season with nutmeg, salt and white pepper. Transfer to a metal bowl and chill until very cold, 10-15 minutes.

Set the chilled bowl in a larger bowl of ice and water. Using a wooden spoon, beat the mixture 1-2 minutes. It will thicken slightly. Beat in the cream by spoonfuls, beating well between additions – the mixture should be very thick. Beat in the peppers with the truffles and their liquid if using.

Bring a small pan of water to the boil and poach a teaspoon of mixture for 1-2 minutes. Taste and adjust the seasoning of the remaining mixture if necessary – it should be highly seasoned. The mixture should hold a shape after poaching; if soft, beat in another egg white and chill very thoroughly.

Pack half of the mixture in the mould or loaf pan. Arrange strips of fish lengthwise on the mixture. Add the remaining mixture, smooth the top and cover with a lid or several layers of foil. Half-fill a roasting pan with water. Set the terrine in the pan and bring the water to the boil on the stove. Transfer to the oven and cook until done, 40-50 minutes.

Meanwhile, make the ginger sauce: in a medium saucepan, melt 2 tablespoons of the butter, add the garlic, onion, shallot, bouquet garni and

ginger and sauté until soft but not browned, 3-5 minutes. Stir in the wine and simmer until reduced by half, 1-2 minutes. Whisk the remaining butter into the sauce a few pieces at a time, working on and off the heat so the butter softens and thickens the sauce without melting to oil. Strain the sauce into another saucepan, pressing the vegetables well to extract all their juices. Taste, adjust the seasoning and keep warm on a rack over a pan of warm water.

Let the cooked terrine stand for 10-15 minutes to reabsorb juices. Run a knife around the edge and turn out. The peppers will have given off water, so dry the terrine's edges with paper towels. Cut it into 1.25-cm/½-inch slices and arrange on a warmed platter or plates. Spoon over a little sauce and serve the rest separately. Decorate with sliced truffles and watercress if you like.

Lobster with shallots and white wine *Homard à la bordelaise*

Lobster is so often served in a pungent américaine sauce with tomato and garlic, and I much prefer this gentle alternative. If possible, use a female lobster as the coral (eggs) will add vivid colour to the sauce.

SERVES 2

**1 whole lobster
(about 750 g/1 ½ pounds)
75 g/2½ oz butter
salt and pepper
2-3 tablespoons Cognac
1 small carrot, very finely diced
(brunoise)
4 shallots, chopped
1 tablespoon flour
250 ml/8 fl oz dry white wine
60 ml/2 fl oz crème fraîche or
double cream
2 tablespoons chopped chervil
or tarragon**

Set the lobster on a chopping board and cover the tail with a cloth. Hold the lobster firmly by the tail. Using the point of a large knife, pierce the shell at the centre of the head all the way down to the chopping board. Continue cutting to split the tail. Turn the lobster around and, holding the head, cut it in half lengthwise. Crack the claw shells, striking them with the back of the knife. Pull out and discard the stomach sac from each half. Remove the green liver (tomalley) and any greenish black coral, chop coarsely and reserve.

Melt half the butter in a sauté pan. Lay the lobster halves, cut-side up, in the pan and season the exposed flesh with salt and pepper. Cover the pan and sauté until the meat is done, 5-7 minutes.

Add the Cognac and carefully flame either with a lighted match or by tilting the pan to catch the gas flame. Remove the lobster halves from pan.

Sauté the carrot and shallots in the pan until soft but not brown, stirring often, for 3-5 minutes. Add the flour and cook for 1 minute. Add the wine and boil, stirring to dissolve the pan juices, until reduced by half, 2-3 minutes. Stir in the cream, reserved liver and coral and simmer, whisking constantly, 30-60 seconds. (The coral turns red when cooked.)

Remove from the heat and add the remaining butter in 2-3 pieces, shaking the pan until the butter is fully incorporated. Stir in half of the chopped herbs, reserving the rest. Taste and adjust seasoning.

Remove the claw meat from the shell. Remove the body meat, pulling it out in pieces. Remove the tail meat and slice it at an angle. Trim and discard the gills

(dead man's fingers) from the underside of the body shell. Set the shells on plates. Place the body meat in the bottom of each shell. Arrange the tail meat inside the shell and set the claw meat in one piece on top. Spoon over the sauce and sprinkle with reserved herbs. If necessary, warm in a low oven for 1-2 minutes, and serve.

Clams on the half-shell with garlic, green pepper and bacon

This recipe, commonly called clams Casino, is equally good made with oysters or large mussels. Here I call for lemon slices to steady the shells on the baking sheet instead of the more usual coarse sea salt, which all too easily strays into the clam shells.

SERVES 4

**24 littleneck or
cherrystone clams**

4 lemons

1 tablespoon vegetable oil

**1 green pepper, cored, seeded
and finely diced**

2 garlic cloves, finely chopped

**6 thin slices of bacon
(about 250 g/½ pound)**

Preheat the oven to 220°C/425°F/gas7. Scrub the clams under cold running water. Shuck the clams: hold each clam in a cloth in the palm of your hand and insert the tip of a small knife between the shells near the hinge. Twist the knife, prying the shells apart. Cut the clam meat from the bottom and top shells. Rinse the bottom shells and set the clam meat back on this half-shell. Squeeze the juice from 1 lemon and slice the remaining lemons – you need 24 slices. Set the shells on a baking sheet on lemon slices to keep them steady.

Heat the oil in a small frying pan, add the green pepper and sauté until soft, 3-5 minutes. Add the garlic and continue cooking until fragrant, 1-2 minutes. Cut the bacon into pieces the same size as the clams.

Sprinkle a little lemon juice over each clam, spoon over the green pepper and garlic and top with a piece of bacon. Bake in the oven until the bacon is crisp and brown and clams are just done, 8-10 minutes. Transfer the clams on the lemon slices to individual plates and serve at once.

Mussel chowder with fennel and saffron

This fish chowder is more of a stew, and makes a generous meal in itself. I like to serve it with sliced baguette, baked in the oven until dry so it forms croûtes for soaking in the fish broth. Any well-flavoured white fish does well here, including cod, haddock, monkfish and hake.

SERVES 4

30 g/1 oz butter

2 small fennel bulbs
(about 375 g/$^3/_4$ pound
in total), sliced

1 onion, chopped

salt and white pepper

750 g/1$^1/_2$ pounds potatoes,
peeled and cut into
2.5-cm/1-inch cubes

250 ml/8 fluid ounces fish stock

large pinch of saffron threads

1 bay leaf

1 kg/2 pounds mussels

500 g/1 pound white
fish fillets, cut into
4-cm/1$^1/_2$-inch chunks

500 ml/16 fl oz milk

250 ml/8 fl oz double cream

2 tablespoons chopped
fresh parsley

Melt the butter in a large soup pot and add the fennel, onion, salt and pepper. Sauté gently, stirring often, until the vegetables are soft but not starting to brown, 10-12 minutes.

Spread the potatoes on the vegetables. Bring the fish stock to a boil, add the saffron and pour the mixture over the potatoes. Add the bay leaf, cover and bring to the boil. Lower the heat and simmer until the potatoes are just tender, 12-15 minutes.

Meanwhile, scrub the mussels under cold running water, pulling off the stringy 'beards'. Discard any mussels that do not close when tapped.

Arrange the fish fillets over the potatoes and add the milk. Stir gently to mix the ingredients and spread the colour of the saffron. Scatter the mussels on top, cover tightly with the lid and simmer very gently until the fish is just tender when flaked with a fork and the mussels have opened, 3-5 minutes. Note that the milk should scarcely simmer – not boil, or it may curdle.

Add the cream and parsley and bring just to the boil. Discard the bay leaf, taste and adjust the seasoning of the chowder. Serve it from the pot, or spooned into warm bowls.

Grilled scallops with prosciutto cream sauce

Deceptively simple, this velvety sauce made with prosciutto and mushrooms is the perfect foil for fresh, sweet scallops. By all means replace the button mushrooms with wild varieties when you can find them.

SERVES 6-8 AS A STARTER, OR 4 AS A
    MAIN COURSE

750 g/1 ½ pounds scallops
30 g/1 oz butter
vegetable oil for the grill rack

FOR THE PROSCIUTTO CREAM SAUCE
75 g/2 ½ oz thinly sliced
    prosciutto
30 g/1 oz butter
1 tablespoon olive oil
1 garlic clove, finely chopped
1 shallot, finely chopped
1 small carrot, very finely diced
    (brunoise)
3 tablespoons white wine
165 g/5 ½ oz button
    mushrooms, diced
60 ml/2 fl oz double cream or
    crème fraîche
30 g/1 oz butter, chilled and cut
    into pieces
salt and pepper
2 tablespoons chopped parsley

Make the prosciutto cream sauce: cut the prosciutto into thin strips about 2 cm/¾ inch long. Heat the butter and olive oil in a saucepan, add the garlic and shallot and sauté until fragrant, 1-2 minutes. Add the carrot and sauté until beginning to soften, 1-2 minutes. Pour over the white wine and boil, stirring, until reduced by half. Stir in the mushrooms and cook until slightly softened, 1-2 minutes. Stir in the cream or crème fraîche with the prosciutto strips and boil until slightly thickened, 1-2 minutes.

Turn the heat to low and gradually whisk in the butter pieces to make a smooth creamy sauce. Work on and off the heat, so that the butter softens and thickens the sauce without melting to oil. Season to taste with salt and pepper. Keep the sauce warm on a rack over a pan of hot but not boiling water.

Preheat the grill. Discard the small crescent-shaped muscles at the sides of the scallops. Rinse the scallops and pat dry with paper towels. Place them on an oiled grill rack, dot with butter and season with salt and pepper. Set the rack about 7.5 cm/3 inches from the heat and grill the scallops until they are just done, 2-3 minutes on each side.

Meanwhile, stir all but 1 teaspoon of the parsley into the sauce. Spoon the sauce on 4 warmed plates, arrange the grilled scallops on top and sprinkle with reserved parsley. Serve at once.

OTHER USES FOR THE PROSCIUTTO CREAM SAUCE
This delicious sauce is extremely versatile and can be served with a wide range of foods, from grilled lobster and firm white fish to veal escalopes and sautéed or grilled chicken breasts. It is also a perfect dressing for asparagus and makes a great pasta sauce, particularly for stuffed pasta containing any of these ingredients.

Maryland steamed crabs

Spicy steamed blue crabs served in the shell – as many as you can eat – are an institution on Maryland's Chesapeake Bay. The flavouring used is equally traditional and here's my version. It is also good for flavouring fish soups and even for sprinkling on fish salads. Crabs steamed this way are delicious on their own, but you may like to give each diner a dipping bowl of melted butter.

SERVES 2-3

12 blue crabs or 2-3 Dungeness
   or common European crabs
750 ml/1 $\frac{1}{4}$ pints flat beer
1 teaspoon ground bay leaf
$\frac{1}{2}$ teaspoon celery salt
$\frac{1}{2}$ teaspoon black pepper
$\frac{1}{2}$ teaspoon dry mustard
$\frac{1}{4}$ teaspoon salt
$\frac{1}{4}$ teaspoon freshly grated
   nutmeg
$\frac{1}{4}$ teaspoon ground ginger
$\frac{1}{4}$ teaspoon ground cloves
$\frac{1}{4}$ teaspoon paprika
$\frac{1}{4}$ teaspoon chilli powder,
   or to taste

Combine the beer with all the dry flavourings in a small pan and bring to the boil.

Put half the crabs in a large pot and pour over half the flavouring liquid. Place the rest of the crabs on top and pour over the remaining liquid. Bring to the boil, cover tightly and reduce the heat. Steam the crabs until done, stirring them once, 20-25 minutes for blue crabs and 30-35 minutes for larger red crabs.

Transfer the crabs to a large warmed serving bowl and provide each person with a nutcracker or mallet for cracking the shell.

MARYLAND STEAMED OR BOILED PRAWNS

These flavourings work equally well with prawns. Make the flavouring liquid in the same way and use to steam or boil whole medium-to-large prawns in their shells just until they turn pink (5-7 minutes for steaming and 3-5 minutes for boiling, even longer if they are really large).

Poultry & game birds

A whole roast or braised chicken is comfort food, and happily within reach of a modest budget. We eat it at least once a week, so I'm expert in dressing up the average bird. Try seasoning the skin and cavity, not just with salt and pepper but with a brushing of soy sauce or white wine and olive oil, or rub the skin with a dry marinade of mustard, ground ginger, nutmeg and paprika

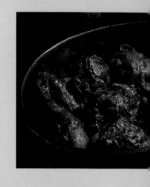

Poached or steamed chicken can be far from plain. From my birthplace in northern England comes 'hindle wakes', simmered chicken stuffed with prunes in a lemon cream sauce. Perhaps my favourite dish of this sort is the archetypal French *poule au pot*, stuffed with herbs, smoked ham, chicken liver and breadcrumbs, and simmered in stock with vegetables.

Pieces of poultry offer another wonderful range of recipes, from simple southern fried chicken or grilled buffalo wings to turkey in a Mexican *mole* sauce flavoured with chocolate and chillies. In Spain, you'll find the Christmas turkey is cut into pieces to simmer with onion, herbs and saffron.

Roast duck with cornbread stuffing, duck with plum sauce, duck braised with sauerkraut or olives, Russian goose with walnut stuffing, Austrian stuffed Christmas goose with apple and prunes – don't the very ideas make you hungry? They do me. I love all those succulent dark-fleshed birds which go so well with tart and fruit flavours. Roasting is the cooking method of choice if you like crisp skin, though braising or pot-roasting will ensure that an elderly bird becomes moist and tender.

Pot-roast chicken with potatoes, bacon and onion

The classic bonne femme garnish of potatoes, bacon and onion makes this dish a meal in itself.

SERVES 4

**1 chicken (about
 1.75 kg/3½ pounds)**
45 g/1½ oz butter
125 g/4 oz lean bacon, diced
**20-24 baby onions, blanched
 and peeled**
**625 g/1¼ pounds potatoes,
 peeled and cut into
 2-cm/¼-inch chunks**
salt and pepper

trussing needle and string

Preheat the oven to 175°C/350°F/gas4. Season the skin and cavity of the chicken with salt and pepper and truss it.

In a flameproof casserole, melt the butter, add the bacon and onions and cook until brown, stirring often, 8-10 minutes. Remove them, add the potato chunks, season with salt and pepper and brown these, 8-10 minutes. Take them out, add the chicken and brown well on all sides, 8-10 minutes.

Set the chicken in the casserole on its back, cover tightly and roast in the oven, turning the bird from time to time, until it is almost tender, 35-45 minutes.

Lift out the chicken and discard excess fat from the casserole if necessary, leaving about 2 tablespoons. Add the browned onions, bacon and potatoes to the bottom of pan and set the chicken on top. Cover and continue cooking until the chicken is done and vegetables are very tender, 15-20 minutes longer.

Discard the trussing strings and set the chicken on a serving platter. Taste the bacon and vegetables, adjust the seasoning if necessary and spoon them around the chicken, together with the cooking juices.

Spatchcock of baby chicken with shallot confit

To 'spatchcock' means to split and flatten a bird for cooking, leaving it joined at the breast. Here I'm suggesting little birds, but you can also spatchcock larger chickens to serve 2 people. Leftover shallot confit keeps well in the refrigerator for up to two weeks.

SERVES 4

4 baby chickens
   (about 500 g/1 pound each)
60 g/2 oz butter
salt and pepper
2 tablespoons Dijon-style mustard

FOR THE SHALLOT CONFIT
500 g/1 pound shallots, peeled
60 ml/2 fl oz white wine
60 ml/2 fl oz white wine vinegar
150 g/5 oz sugar
½ teaspoon salt

8 wooden or metal skewers

Split and flatten the birds: cut the backbones and wing-tips from the birds with shears or scissors. Snip the wishbones to sever them. Flatten the birds with the palm of your hand, breaking the breastbone. Make a small incision between each leg and the bottom end of the breastbone and pass through the ends of the legs to hold them in place. Thread a skewer through the wings to hold them flat. Thread a second skewer through the legs.

Make the shallot confit: slice the shallots very thinly. Put the wine, vinegar, sugar, salt and a little pepper in a large pan and heat gently, stirring from time to time, until the sugar dissolves. Bring just to the boil and stir in the shallots. Cover and cook over very low heat, stirring often, until the shallots are translucent and very tender, 20-25 minutes. Taste and adjust the seasoning.

Meanwhile, preheat the grill and brush the rack with oil. Melt the butter and brush the birds with half of it. Season them and put on the grill rack, skin side up, about 7.5 cm/3 inches from the heat. Grill for about 10 minutes, basting occasionally with butter. Turn them over, baste with the remaining butter and grill for about 10 minutes more. Turn them again and brush with mustard. Grill, skin side up, until done, about 10 minutes more.

To serve: remove the skewers and arrange the birds on individual plates. Spoon some confit beside the birds and serve the rest separately.

Sauté of chicken with paprika

A few spoonfuls of sour cream set off the brilliant red of the paprika sauce. Fresh noodles are a classic accompaniment.

SERVES 4

1 chicken (about 1.4 kg/3 pounds), cut into 6 pieces
salt and pepper
2 tablespoons sweet red paprika
2 tablespoons vegetable oil
1 onion, chopped
175 ml/6 fl oz chicken stock, more if needed
3 red sweet peppers
2 tablespoons tomato purée
75 ml/2½ fl oz sour cream, double cream or crème fraîche

Season the pieces of chicken with salt and pepper. Sprinkle them with paprika, patting it on with your hands until thoroughly coated. Heat the oil in a sauté or frying pan. Beginning with the legs, add the chicken pieces, skin side down. When they begin to brown, add the wing pieces and finally the breasts. (Note: do not use too high a heat or the paprika may scorch.) When all the pieces are well browned, turn them over and brown them on the other sides, 8-10 minutes in total.

Remove the chicken from the pan and add the onion. Sauté until soft but not browned, 3-4 minutes. Return the chicken to pan and add half of the stock. Cover tightly and cook over low heat until the chicken is done, 30-35 minutes. Add more stock during cooking if the pan gets too dry.

Meanwhile, roast the peppers either over an open flame or under a preheated grill, turning them until the skin chars and bursts, 7-10 minutes. Put them in a plastic bag to allow them to steam and the skin to loosen, and leave to cool. Peel the cooled peppers, discard their cores and seeds, and cut the flesh into strips.

When the chicken is cooked, remove the pieces from the pan. By now, the pan juices should be reduced to a glaze; if not, boil them well to reduce them. Discard any fat from pan, stir in the tomato purée and the remaining stock, and bring just back to the boil. Return the chicken pieces to the pan together with the pepper strips and heat gently, 1-2 minutes. Taste the sauce and adjust the seasoning, if necessary.

Arrange the chicken on a warmed platter or on individual plates and spoon the sauce on top. Spoon over the cream or crème fraîche as a contrast to the sauce and serve at once.

Poached chicken with salsify and cream

All the ingredients in this traditional Normandy wedding dish are white. You may substitute baby turnip or celeriac for the salsify, a slender root which resembles white asparagus in shape and flavour.

SERVES 4

**1 chicken or boiling fowl
    (about 1.8 kg/4 pounds)
salt and white pepper
1 onion, studded with
    2 cloves
2 carrots, quartered
2 garlic cloves
bouquet garni, including tarragon
300 ml/$\frac{1}{2}$ pint white wine
2 litres/3 $\frac{1}{4}$ pints chicken stock or
    water, more if needed
1 kg/2 pounds salsify**

FOR THE CREAM SAUCE

**75 g/2$\frac{1}{2}$ oz butter
45 g/1$\frac{1}{2}$ oz flour
375 ml/12 fl oz crème fraîche or
    double cream**

trussing needle and string

Season the skin and cavity of the bird, and truss it. Put it in a pot into which it fits quite tightly, together with the onion, carrots, garlic and bouquet garni. Pour in the wine and enough chicken stock or water just to cover, add a little salt and pepper and bring to the boil. Cover and simmer over low heat, skimming occasionally, until the bird is done, 1-1$\frac{1}{4}$ hours for chicken and 1$\frac{1}{2}$-2 hours for boiling fowl.

About 30 minutes before the end of cooking, peel the salsify and cut it in 5-cm/2-inch lengths. Put it in a pan and add enough stock from the bird to cover it generously. Cover and simmer until tender, 25-35 minutes. Drain and return the stock to the pot.

When the bird is done, transfer to a cutting board. Discard the strings and cover the bird with foil to keep it warm. Skim any fat from surface of stock and measure 1 litre/1$\frac{2}{3}$ pints. Boil this until reduced to 750 ml/1$\frac{1}{4}$ pints.

Make the cream sauce: melt the butter in a pan, whisk in the flour and cook until foaming. Strain in the reduced stock, stir and bring to the boil, whisking constantly until the sauce thickens, 1-2 minutes. Simmer for 2 minutes, then add the crème fraîche or cream. Taste and adjust the seasoning. Continue simmering the sauce until it lightly coats the back of a spoon, 3-5 minutes.

Add the salsify to the sauce and heat gently for 1-2 minutes. Carve the chicken into 6-8 pieces and arrange it on a platter. Spoon the salsify and some sauce around the chicken and serve the rest separately.

Chicken breast on horseback with tarragon velouté

**Pungent tarragon is a pick-me-up for this chicken
breast served on a crisp potato cake.**

SERVES 4

**4 boneless chicken breasts,
    without skin
500 g/1 lb baking potatoes
60 ml/2 fl oz double cream
salt and white pepper**

FOR THE TARRAGON VELOUTÉ
**large bunch of tarragon
1 litre/1^2/$_3$ pints chicken stock
60 g/2 oz butter
30 g/1 oz flour
juice of $\frac{1}{2}$ lemon, or to taste**

Preheat the oven to 175°C/350°F/gas4. Start the sauce: strip half the tarragon leaves from the stems, reserving the stems and 4 small sprigs for decoration. Chop the leaves and set aside. In a saucepan, bring the stock to the boil with the remaining tarragon and reserved stems.

Arrange the chicken breasts in a medium baking dish, then pour over the stock and its tarragon. Cover with buttered foil and bake until tender when pierced with a fork, 15-20 minutes. Remove them to a plate and cover with foil to keep warm. Reserve the cooking liquid. Increase the oven setting to 200°C/400°F/gas6.

Meanwhile, make the potato cakes: peel the potatoes and coarsely grate them using a food processor or grater. Squeeze in a cloth to remove water and put them in a large bowl. Stir in the cream, salt and pepper. Note: work quickly or the potatoes will discolour. Brush a baking sheet with vegetable oil and add the potatoes in 4 mounds. With a spatula, flatten them into 6-mm/1/4-inch thick cakes. Bake in the preheated oven until brown, 12-15 minutes, then turn and continue baking until crisp, 12-15 minutes more.

Finish the tarragon velouté sauce: melt the butter in a heavy-based pan, whisk in the flour and cook until foaming but not browned, 30-60 seconds. Whisk in the reserved cooking liquid, with the tarragon stems, and bring to the boil, whisking constantly until it thickens. Season lightly – the flavour will concentrate as the sauce reduces. Simmer until done, skimming occasionally, 15-30 minutes.

Strain the sauce into another pan, bring just to the boil and stir in the chopped tarragon and lemon juice. Taste and adjust the seasoning. Place the potato cakes on 4 individual plates. Slice the chicken breasts at an angle and arrange in a fan shape over the cakes. Partially coat the chicken with sauce and top with a tarragon sprig. Serve at once, passing the remaining sauce separately.

Moroccan roast turkey with honey and almond glaze

Basting with a honey-and-almond glaze keeps this turkey moist and makes the skin deliciously crisp and dark golden-brown. Couscous is a good accompaniment, flavoured with saffron and raisins if you like.

SERVES 8

1 turkey (about 4.5 kg/10
    pounds), with giblets
2 tablespoons sesame seeds
175 g/6 oz blanched almonds,
    very finely chopped
2 tablespoons ground
    cinnamon
1 tablespoon ground cumin
1 tablespoon ground coriander
2 teaspoons ground ginger
1 teaspoon ground cloves
1 teaspoon salt
1 teaspoon pepper
1 onion, studded with 6 whole
    cloves
30 g/1 oz butter, softened
2 cinnamon sticks
125 ml/4 fl oz honey
500 ml/16 fl oz chicken stock,
    more if needed

trussing needle and string

Preheat the oven to 175°C/350°F/gas4. Spread the sesame seeds and chopped almonds in a single layer in a shallow pan and roast them, shaking the pan occasionally, until golden, 8-10 minutes. Set aside to cool.

In a small bowl, mix the ground cinnamon, cumin, coriander, ginger and cloves with the salt and pepper. Rub both the skin and cavity of the turkey with this mixture. Put the onion studded with the cloves in the cavity and truss the bird. Place the bird on its back in a roasting pan and spread the skin with softened butter. Cut the giblets into pieces and add them to the pan with the cinnamon sticks. Combine the honey and half the stock and pour this over the bird.

Roast the bird in the preheated oven, turning it on one side, then the other, and then returning it to its back, until done, 2½ -3 hours. Baste often and, when the stock and honey begin to brown, add the remaining stock.

About 15 minutes before the turkey is due to be done, remove it from the roasting pan and strain the pan juices into a small saucepan. Skim off the fat and boil the juices to reduce them if necessary – there should be about 250 ml/8 fl oz of this glaze. Stir in the toasted sesame seeds and almonds. Return the turkey to the roasting pan, spread the glaze over the top and continue roasting, basting very often, until the skin is dark golden brown and crisp, 10-15 minutes.

Discard the trussing strings. Transfer the turkey to a warmed serving plate, spoon over any remaining glaze, cover with foil and leave to stand for 10-15 minutes before carving.

Lemon roast duck with olives and capers

This recipe borrows flavours from the Mediterranean to update classic *canard à l'orange*. A *gastrique*, made by dissolving caramelized sugar in vinegar, enlivens many fruit sauces like this.

SERVES 3-4

1 duck (about 2 kg/4$\frac{1}{2}$ pounds),
  with giblets
salt and pepper
2 lemons
3-4 bay leaves
$\frac{1}{2}$ teaspoon whole cloves
4 tablespoons olive oil

FOR THE SAUCE
60 g/2 oz sugar
4 tablespoons water
75 ml/2$\frac{1}{2}$ fl oz wine vinegar
750 ml/1$\frac{1}{4}$ pints chicken stock
1 onion, diced
1 carrot, diced
2 tablespoons flour
60 g/2 oz mild brine- or oil-
  cured black olives
1 tablespoon capers, rinsed and
  drained

trussing needle and string

Preheat the oven to 230°C/450°F/gas8. Season the skin and cavity of the duck and prick the skin so that the fat escapes during roasting. Pare the zest from the lemons and put this inside the duck, together with the bay leaves and cloves. Truss the duck, place it on its back in a roasting pan and rub the skin with olive oil and the juice of 1 of the lemons. Cut the giblets into pieces and add them to the pan.

Roast the duck in the oven until it starts to sizzle, about 15 minutes. Reduce the setting to 200°C/400°F/gas6, turn the duck on one side, baste and roast for 15 minutes. Turn it on its other side, baste and roast for 15 minutes more. Finally return the duck to its back and roast, basting often, until done to taste, 1-1$\frac{3}{4}$ hours.

For the sauce, prepare a caramel-vinegar gastrique: in a small pan, heat the sugar in the water until it has dissolved, then boil steadily to a light-brown caramel. Remove the pan from the heat and at once add vinegar. (Note: stand well back, because vapour from the vinegar will sting your eyes.) Heat the gastrique gently until the caramel is dissolved. Add the stock and the juice of the remaining lemon. Bring to the boil and simmer until reduced, 3-5 minutes.

Transfer the cooked duck to a warmed serving plate. Cover with foil and let stand for 10-15 minutes. Pour off all but 1 tablespoon of fat from the roasting pan. Add the onion and carrot to the giblets and cook until well browned, 5-7 minutes. Stir in the flour and cook, stirring, until well browned, 1-2 minutes. Pour in the gastrique and bring to the boil, stirring to dissolve the pan juices. Simmer until slightly thickened, 4-5 minutes. Strain into a saucepan, pressing to extract all the liquid. Simmer until the sauce is glossy and lightly coats the back of a spoon, 4-5 minutes.

Add the olives and capers to the sauce. Heat gently without boiling, taste and adjust seasoning. Spoon a little sauce over the duck and serve the rest separately.

Magret of duck with green peppercorn sauce

Magret is the French name for boneless duck breast, traditionally the plump meat on a bird which has been flattened for foie gras. The legs of the bird are used for confit.

SERVES 2

**1 large or 2 small boneless
duck breasts
(about 375 g/12 oz)**
1 tablespoon oil
salt and pepper

FOR THE GREEN PEPPERCORN
SAUCE
3 shallots, finely chopped
375 ml/12 fl oz red wine
**60 ml/2 fl oz brown beef or veal
stock**
**2 tablespoons crème fraîche or
double cream**
**1 teaspoon green peppercorns,
drained and crushed**
1 tablespoon butter

Heat the oil in a heavy frying pan. Season the duck breast(s) on both sides with salt and pepper, and score the skin so the fat will escape during cooking. Fry skin side down over high heat until the skin is well browned, 3-5 minutes. Turn the breast(s) over, lower the heat to medium and continue frying until cooked to your taste, 3-7 minutes. Transfer to a carving board and keep warm.

Make the green peppercorn sauce: discard all but a tablespoon of fat from the pan. Add the chopped shallots and sauté for 1 minute. Add the red wine, whisk to dissolve the pan juices and boil until reduced by half. Whisk in the stock and boil to concentrate the flavour if necessary. Add the cream and peppercorns and simmer for 2-3 minutes.

Carve the duck breast(s) into slices at an angle and arrange on 2 warmed plates. (The skin can be discarded if you prefer.) Drain any juice from the duck into the sauce. Take the sauce from the heat and add the butter in 2-3 pieces, shaking the pan until the butter is fully incorporated. Taste the sauce and adjust the seasoning. Spoon over the duck and serve at once.

Beer-roast goose with prune stuffing

Dark beer helps crisp the skin and adds a mellow depth to the gravy. The bird is likely to render cupfuls of fat during cooking so keep it for frying potatoes another time.

SERVES 5-6

1 goose
   (about 4.5 kg/9-10 pounds)
250 ml/8 fl oz dark beer
30 g/1 oz softened butter

FOR THE STUFFING
boiling water to cover
250 g/8 oz pitted prunes
liver from the goose
15 g/$\frac{1}{2}$ oz butter
2 shallots, chopped
250 g/$\frac{1}{2}$ pound minced pork,
   fat and lean mixed
salt and pepper
90 g/3 oz fresh white
   breadcrumbs
4 tablespoons chopped fresh
   parsley

FOR THE GRAVY
15 g/$\frac{1}{2}$ oz flour
250 ml/8 fl oz dark beer
500 ml/16 fl oz chicken stock

string for trussing

First make the stuffing: pour boiling water over the prunes to cover and let soften for about 15 minutes. Drain and coarsely chop them. Chop the goose liver. Heat the butter in a frying pan, add the shallots and cook for 1 minute. Stir in the pork and chopped liver with some salt and pepper and cook, stirring constantly, until no longer pink, 3-5 minutes. Take from the heat and stir in the prunes, breadcrumbs and parsley. Adjust the seasoning. The stuffing can be kept in the refrigerator for up to a day.

Preheat the oven to 230°C/150°F/gas8. Wipe the inside of the bird with paper towels, and season the outside. Fill the goose with the stuffing and truss it. Put on a rack in a roasting pan and pour over the beer, rubbing it well into the skin.

Roast the goose until it starts to brown, about 40 minutes. Prick the skin to release the fat under it, then turn bird breast downwards and baste. Lower oven to 180°C/350°F/gas4 and roast for another hour, basting often. Generous amounts of fat will accumulate in the bottom of the pan and you should drain off the excess. Finally, turn the goose once more, so it is breast up. Continue roasting and basting until the bird is very brown, the meat pulls away from the drumstick and juices run clear when you prick the thigh with a skewer, about 1 to 1¼ hours longer. A meat thermometer inserted in the thigh should register 74°C/165°F. If the skin starts to brown too much during cooking, cover loosely with foil.

When the goose is cooked, spread it with the butter and turn the oven back up to 230°C/450°F/gas8. Set the bird on a piece of foil on a baking sheet and put it back in the oven for 5 to 10 minutes to crisp up the skin.

Meanwhile make the gravy: pour all but 2 tablespoons fat from the roasting pan. Stir in the flour and cook for 1-2 minutes until browned. Add the beer, bring to the boil on the stove and simmer, stirring constantly to dissolve the pan juices, 1-2 minutes. Add the stock and simmer until well-flavoured and concentrated, 3 to 5 minutes. Adjust the seasoning and strain it into a bowl to serve separately. Carve the bird at the table.

Braised pheasant with lentils

The green lentils from Le Puy, in the volcanic mountains of central France, are renowned. This recipe is also excellent with guinea fowl or rabbit.

SERVES 4

**2 pheasants, each about
    750 g/1½ pounds
1 tablespoon oil
15 g/½ oz butter
250 g/½ pound bacon, diced
1 onion, chopped
1 carrot, diced
bouquet garni
250 ml/8 fl oz white wine
250 ml/8 fl oz chicken stock,
    more if needed
salt and pepper**

FOR THE LENTILS

**250 g/8 oz Le Puy or other
    dark green lentils
1 onion, studded with a clove
1 garlic clove
bouquet garni**

trussing needle and string

Preheat the oven to 190°C/375°F/gas 5. Truss the pheasant. Heat the oil and butter in a heavy flameproof casserole, add the bacon and fry until lightly browned. Remove the bacon, add the pheasants and brown well. Add the onion and carrot and cook over medium heat until soft, 5-7 minutes.

Return the bacon to the casserole with the bouquet garni, wine, stock, salt and pepper. Bring just to the boil, cover and braise in the oven until done to taste, 1-1½ hours. basting occasionally and adding more stock if the pan is dry.

Pick over the lentils, discarding any stones, and wash them well. Put them in a pan with the clove-studded onion, the garlic and bouquet garni, together with enough water to cover them generously. Bring to the boil and skim off any scum. Partially cover and simmer until the lentils are tender and most of the water is absorbed, 30-45 minutes. Stir occasionally, and add more water if the lentils get dry. At the end of cooking they should be moist but not soupy. If too wet, drain off excess liquid. Discard the onion, garlic and bouquet garni.

Remove the cooked pheasants from the casserole. Discard the strings and bouquet garni, and strain the cooking juices into a pan, reserving the bacon and vegetables. Transfer the lentils to the casserole and stir in the bacon and vegetables. Adjust the seasoning and cook over a low heat for about 10 minutes to blend the flavours.

Meanwhile, cut the pheasants in half, discarding their backbones, and trim the wing-tips and ends of the legs. Place the pheasant halves on top of the lentils. Discard excess fat from reserved cooking juices and, if necessary, boil them to concentrate the flavour. Taste and adjust the seasoning.

Serve the pheasants and lentils from the casserole or transfer them to a platter. Spoon some cooking juices on top of the pheasants and serve the rest separately.

Braised pigeons with 40 cloves of garlic

You'll be amazed how this large amount of garlic blends and mellows while the pigeon braises in the oven. Young, farm-raised pigeons cook quite quickly and can be served rare, but wild or older birds need longer cooking. Serve the pigeons, one per person, with roasted or glazed root vegetables such as turnips, carrots, root celery, baby beetroots and potatoes.

SERVES 4

3-4 whole heads of garlic

4 whole pigeons, trussed

salt and pepper

6-8 sprigs of fresh thyme

30 g/1 oz butter

500 ml/16 fl oz chicken stock, plus more if needed

Preheat the oven to 190°C/375°F/gas5. Separate the garlic heads into cloves, leaving them unpeeled. Season the pigeons with salt and pepper and push a thyme sprig in each cavity.

Heat the butter in a large casserole, add the pigeons and brown them on all sides over medium heat, taking about 10 minutes. Set the birds breast upwards. Add the garlic cloves and remaining thyme, together with enough stock to half-cover the pigeons. Bring to the boil, cover the pan and braise in the oven until the pigeons are very tender when pierced in the thigh with a two-pronged fork, 30-40 minutes if they are young and you prefer them rare, or up to 1½ hours for tough older birds. Check from time to time during cooking and if the pan seems dry, add more stock.

Transfer the pigeons to a serving dish, cover and keep warm. Squash a garlic clove: if it is very soft, drain about half the cloves and pile them around the birds. If the garlic is still firm, simmer it on top of the stove until tender, then remove half the cloves. Work the remaining garlic with the cooking liquid through a strainer into a small saucepan, pressing well to extract all the garlic pulp and form a sauce. Bring to the boil and, if necessary, simmer the sauce to reduce it until slightly thickened. Taste and adjust the seasoning.

Discard the trussing strings from the pigeons but leave the garlic cloves in their skins for guests to squeeze out the soft pulp. Serve the sauce in a separate bowl.

Winemaker's pheasant en cocotte

In this recipe, mature wild pheasants will take at least an hour - or even two - to cook until they are tender. However, when farm-raised, tenderness is guaranteed and they can be cooked just until they are still rare and juicy. If you use seedless grapes, you'll avoid the tiresome job of deseeding them. Braised fennel or celery and small boiled potatoes in their skins make good accompaniments.

SERVES 4

2 pheasants (each about 750 g/1 ½ pounds)
4 slices of streaky bacon
60 g/2 oz butter
3 tablespoons marc or Cognac

FOR THE SAUCE

175 g/6 oz seedless green grapes
175 g/6 oz seedless red grapes
250 ml/8 fl oz dry white wine, such as Sauvignon Blanc
250 ml/8 fl oz chicken stock
2 teaspoons arrowroot mixed to a paste with 2 tablespoons cold water
2-3 teaspoons marc or Cognac

Preheat the oven to 190°C/375°F/gas5. Set aside the pheasants' giblets and wipe the birds with damp paper towels. Sprinkle them inside and out with salt and pepper and truss them. Cover the breasts with bacon and tie it with string.

Heat half the butter in a casserole and brown the pheasants thoroughly on all sides over medium heat, taking about 10 minutes.

Add the giblets and cover the casserole. Cook in the oven until the juices poured from the centre of the birds runs pink but not red, 25-30 minutes. If you prefer your birds well done or if they are tough, continue cooking until the juice runs clear and they are tender when pierced with a skewer.

Meanwhile, put the grapes for the sauce in a pan with the wine and simmer until lightly cooked but not soft, 1-2 minutes. Set them aside.

When the pheasants are cooked, pour off excess fat, add the marc to the pan and flambé it. Take the birds from the pan, discard the bacon and the trussing strings. Using scissors, cut along each side of the backbone and remove it. Cut the birds in half along the breast bone and trim the leg bones to neaten them. Arrange the halves overlapping on a serving dish and keep them warm.

To make the sauce: add the wine from cooking the grapes to the pot and boil it until reduced by about half, stirring to dissolve pan juices. Add the stock, bring to the boil and strain it into a saucepan. Bring the liquid to a boil and whisk in the arrowroot paste to make a sauce that lightly coats a spoon. Add the grapes and reheat them gently. Stir the marc into the sauce, taste, and adjust the seasoning.

Spoon the sauce and grapes over the pheasants and serve.

Meat & game

I am happy to say I'm of the generation that remembers
Sunday lunch with roast beef and Yorkshire pudding
with plenty of crispy trimmings. Accompaniments are
just as traditional as the roast itself. In France, lamb
demands fresh haricots verts, dried flageolet beans and
a creamy potato gratin; whereas in England, baby boiled
potatoes and mint sauce are more likely. Roast venison
evokes dark wine sauces warm with cracked pepper
and cinnamon, offset by purées of chestnut, pumpkin,
celeriac and perhaps a poached pear.

Long before it reaches the plate, a grand roast of
meat tantalizes the eye and the nose. Among my
favourites are pecan-smoked rack of lamb from the
American South, Breton roast leg of lamb with white

beans and tomato, Swedish roast saddle of venison with sour cream, juniper and redcurrant jelly, and maple venison ham from Canada, not forgetting the international beef Wellington with liver pâté baked in pastry and served with truffle sauce.

When it comes to a family feast, I hope you'll agree that pork wins hands down. Stuffed with garlic, onion and herbs, then basted constantly as it cooks with wine and meat juices, pork is fit for a king. Pigs are now bred to be lean, so the meat dries all the more easily. I prefer a cut which includes the bone to keep it moist such as fresh leg, or loin including the ribs. By itself, barbecued or roast pork can be a bit plain. I like to sweeten it with dried figs or prunes, or flavour it with orange or cranberry. Roast pork goes well with hot pepper jelly, apple sauce, roast garlic and mashed potatoes.

Roast fillet of beef with coffee pan gravy

It was the cooks of the American South who first thought of using coffee to flavour their ham gravy. Now some modern French chefs have taken up the practice with delicious results. Unusual flavourings for gravy include a tablespoon of whole-grain mustard, whisked in after straining the gravy. A tablespoon of toasted sesame seeds plus a few drops of dark sesame oil will add Oriental depth, as will a teaspoon of soy sauce, but the effect should be subtle, so don't overdo it.

SERVES 4

1.15-kg/2$\frac{1}{2}$-pound piece of beef fillet

salt and pepper

2 tablespoons vegetable oil

250 ml/8 fl oz brown beef or veal stock

2 tablespoons coffee beans

250 ml/8 fl oz black coffee

2 tablespoons bourbon whiskey (optional)

2 tablespoons cold butter, cut into pieces

trussing string

Preheat the oven to 260°C/500°F/gas10 or to its highest possible setting. Trim any sinew, membrane or excess fat from the beef fillet. Fold under the tapered end to give the roast an even cylindrical shape and tie the roast neatly at regular intervals. Measure the diameter of the roast with a ruler. Note: the cooking time is much better gauged by measuring the thickness of the fillet than by using its weight.

Season the beef. Heat the oil in a roasting pan and brown the roast on all sides over high heat, 5-7 minutes. Transfer to the oven and roast until done to taste, 8-9 minutes per 2.5 cm/1 inch for rare meat, 9-10 minutes for medium-cooked and 10-12 minutes for well done. About 5 minutes before the roast is due to be done, pour half the stock over the meat, but stand back as the stock will sputter.

Coarsely chop the coffee beans, pulsing them 2-3 times in a coffee grinder. Alternatively, put the beans in a plastic bag and crush lightly with a rolling pin.

When the beef is done, transfer the pan to the top of the stove. Set the meat on a platter and cover with foil to keep warm. Add the coffee, whiskey if using and the remaining stock to the roasting pan, and bring to the boil, stirring to dissolve the pan juices. Add the coffee beans to the pan and boil to reduce and concentrate flavour, 8-10 minutes. Strain this gravy, bring it back to the boil, taste and adjust the seasoning with salt and pepper. Take the pan from the heat, add the pieces of cold butter and shake the pan to swirl the gravy until the butter is melted and incorporated. Discard the trussing strings from the meat, moisten the meat with a little gravy and serve the rest separately.

Steak with red wine sauce

Chefs have abandoned the traditional espagnole sauce, which took days to make, but reduction by simmering remains the key to a glossy, mellow brown sauce. Even the bare 20 minutes called for here makes a difference.

SERVES 4

2 sirloin steaks (about 750 g/1½ pounds), cut 2.5 cm/1 inch thick

2 tablespoons oil

salt and pepper

bunch of watercress for decoration

FOR THE RED WINE SAUCE

30 g/1 oz butter

3 shallots, finely chopped

500 ml/16 fl oz red wine

½ teaspoon coarsely ground black pepper

¼ teaspoon freshly grated nutmeg

375 ml/12 fl oz brown veal or beef stock

1 teaspoon arrowroot or potato starch mixed to a paste with 1 tablespoon cold water

Brush the steaks with oil, season both sides with pepper and leave to marinate.

Start the red wine sauce: melt half the butter in a heavy-based saucepan, add the shallots and sauté gently until soft, 2-3 minutes. Add the wine, black pepper and nutmeg, and boil until reduced by half. In another saucepan, bring the stock just to the boil and strain the red wine reduction into it. Simmer to reduce the sauce again by about half, 15-20 minutes.

Meanwhile, preheat the grill. Season the steaks on both sides with salt and set them on the grill rack. Grill about 5 cm/2 inches away from the heat, cooking the steaks to taste, 6-10 minutes, turning them once halfway through cooking.

Finish the sauce: bring the sauce back to the boil and whisk in just enough arrowroot or potato starch paste to thicken it slightly. Remove the pan from the heat, taste the sauce and adjust the seasoning. Add the remaining butter, cut into pieces, swirling the pan so that butter is incorporated smoothly into sauce.

To serve: cut the steaks in diagonal slices, discarding any fat, and arrange on a warmed platter or individual plates. Spoon a little sauce over the steaks. Decorate with watercress and serve at once, with the remaining sauce passed separately.

Roast veal with sorrel and spinach purée

Rôti de veau à la purée d'oseille et d'épinards

I use boneless loin or round of veal for roasting, but breast is also good – and cheaper. If sorrel is not available, you can substitute watercress, boiling the leaves with the spinach.

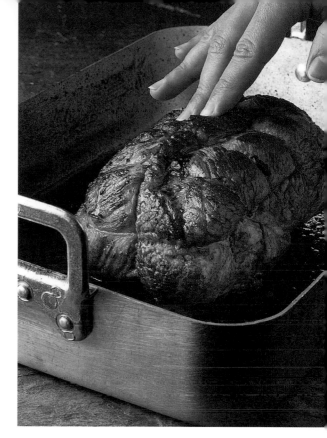

SERVES 6-8

**I veal roast as above
    (about 1.25 kg/2½ pounds)
125-g/4-oz pork or bacon fat,
    cut into short strips
salt and pepper
2 tablespoons vegetable oil
I carrot, thinly sliced
I onion, sliced
175 ml/6 fl oz white wine
175 ml/6 fl oz brown beef or
    veal stock, more if needed**

**FOR THE SORREL AND SPINACH
    PURÉE
750 g/1½ pounds sorrel, well
    washed and stems discarded
750 g/1½ pounds spinach, well
    washed and stems discarded
30 g/1 oz butter
175 ml/6 fl oz double cream**

trussing string

Preheat the oven to 175°C/350°F/gas4. Lard the veal (to keep it moist); pierce with the point of a sharp knife and insert a strip of fat into each incision. Roll into a neat cylinder and tie at regular intervals. Season.

Heat the oil in a roasting pan and brown the veal on all sides. Add the carrot and onion, and stir-fry until lightly browned, 3-5 minutes. Add the wine and boil to reduce by half. Stir in the stock. Roast until done to taste, 1-1¼ hours. Baste often and add more stock, if needed.

Meanwhile, make the purée: put the sorrel in a large pan with a little salt, cover and cook over high heat until wilted, stirring once or twice, 3-5 minutes. Add the butter and cream and cook, stirring, until it thickens to a purée which falls easily from the spoon, about 5 minutes. Pack the spinach into another pan with 2 cm/¾ inch water. Cover and cook over high heat until it starts to wilt. Stir, cover and cook until completely wilted, 1-2 minutes. Drain, let cool, then press out excess water. Chop and stir into the purée. Taste and adjust the seasoning.

Transfer the veal to a carving board and cover with foil. Boil the strained cooking juices to reduce to a gravy. Carve the veal into 1.25-cm/½-inch slices. Reheat the purée and pile on a warmed serving dish. Arrange the veal on top. Serve with the gravy.

Braised leg of lamb with garlic and wild mushrooms

Here I use my favourite wild mushroom – the cep – but feel free to substitute whichever type happens to be available and fresh. You can economize by substituting cultivated mushrooms for part or all of the wild ones.

SERVES 6-8

**1 leg of lamb
   (about 2.25 kg/5 pounds)
4 garlic cloves, peeled and cut
   into slivers
salt and pepper
3 tablespoons oil
15 g/$\frac{1}{2}$ oz butter
2 onions, sliced
2 carrots, sliced
1 celery stalk, sliced
500 g/1 pound ceps, sliced
bunch of thyme
bunch of rosemary
375 ml/12 fl oz white wine
500 ml/16 fl oz brown beef or
   veal stock, more if needed
175 ml/6 fl oz double cream or
   crème fraîche
2 tablespoons chopped parsley**

Preheat the oven to 175°C/350°F/gas4. With the point of a small knife, make several incisions in the lamb and insert slivers of garlic in them. Season the lamb with some salt and pepper.

Heat 2 tablespoons of the oil and the butter in a large flameproof casserole. Brown the lamb on all sides and transfer to a tray. Add the onion, carrot and celery to the casserole, and sauté until browned, 5-7 minutes. With a slotted spoon, transfer these to the tray.

Heat the remaining oil until very hot, add the ceps and sauté, stirring, until they give up their liquid. When this liquid begins to reduce, remove the mushrooms with the slotted spoon and set aside.

Return the onion, carrot and celery to the casserole with the thyme and rosemary. Set the lamb on top, pour over the white wine and simmer for 1 or 2 minutes. Add the stock, bring to the boil, cover and transfer to the preheated oven. Braise the lamb until done to your taste, 2-2$\frac{1}{2}$ hours. Baste the lamb occasionally and add more stock if the casserole gets dry.

When the lamb is done, transfer it to a cutting board and cover with foil to keep warm. Strain the braising liquid, skim off any fat and return it to the casserole. Bring to the boil and, if necessary, boil to reduce to about 250 ml/8 fl oz. Stir the cream into the sauce, add the mushrooms and simmer until they are tender, 2-3 minutes. Taste, adjust seasoning and stir in the chopped parsley.

Carve the lamb and replace the slices on the bone or arrange them on a warmed serving platter. Spoon the mushrooms and some sauce around the sides of the meat and serve the rest separately.

Spicy lamb stew with almond and coconut _Badami roghan josh_

This dark sauce from northern India goes equally well with lamb or beef. Serve the stew with rice pilaf or Indian naan bread (see page 146).

SERVES 3-4

1 kg/2 pounds boned shoulder
    of lamb, cut into 2.5-cm
    1-inch pieces
salt and pepper
75 ml/2½ fl oz vegetable oil
1 teaspoon whole cloves
2 small dried red chilli peppers
1 teaspoon whole peppercorns
2 onions, finely chopped

FOR THE ALMOND AND
    COCONUT SAUCE
60 g/2 oz blanched flaked
    almonds
2 teaspoons ground cumin
1 tablespoon ground coriander
2 tablespoons unsweetened
    grated coconut
4 garlic cloves, cut into pieces
2.5-cm/1-inch piece of fresh
    ginger, chopped
1 teaspoon ground allspice
125 ml/4 fl oz brown beef or veal
    stock, plus more if needed
1 tablespoon tomato paste
75 ml/2½ fl oz plain yoghurt

Trim the lamb of most of the fat. Season the pieces with salt and pepper. Heat the oil in a flameproof casserole, add the cloves, chilli peppers and peppercorns, and heat gently, stirring until the spices are fragrant and infuse the oil, 3-5 minutes. Using a slotted spoon, transfer the spices to a food processor. Increase the heat to high, add the lamb to the casserole in 2-3 batches and brown well on all sides. Remove the lamb to a plate, add the onions to the casserole and sauté until well browned, stirring occasionally, 5-7 minutes.

Meanwhile, make the almond and coconut sauce: chop half the almonds, reserving the rest. Heat a heavy frying pan over a low heat for 3-5 minutes. Add the cumin, coriander, coconut and chopped almonds and roast, stirring, until the spices are fragrant and the nuts are golden, 5-7 minutes. Add the roasted spices and nuts to those in food processor together with the garlic, ginger, allspice and stock. Process until smooth.

Stir the sauce and tomato paste into the browned onions in the casserole and simmer, stirring to dissolve pan juices, 5 minutes. Stir in the yoghurt. Return the meat to the casserole, bring to the boil, cover and simmer, stirring occasionally, until done, 1-1¼ hours. If the casserole gets dry, add more stock. Note: the yoghurt will separate but this is intentional here.

When the lamb is done, taste the sauce and adjust the seasoning. Transfer the stew to a warmed serving bowl or serve directly from the casserole, sprinkled with the reserved almonds.

Roast pork loin with figs and port

Look for figs that are still a bit firm so they bake well, giving up generous juices for the rich sauce. A pilaf of wild rice makes an excellent accompaniment.

SERVES 6

1 rolled pork loin roast (about 1 kg/2 pounds)
salt and pepper
2 teaspoons ground cinnamon
8 large figs (about 375 g/$^3/_4$ pound)
15 g/$^1/_2$ oz butter
1 tablespoon vegetable oil
250 ml/8 fl oz brown beef or veal stock, plus more if needed
250 ml/8 fl oz port
1 tablespoon brown sugar
2 tablespoons redcurrant jelly
juice of $^1/_2$ lemon
1$^1/_2$ teaspoons cornflour, mixed to a paste with 2 tablespoons cold water

trussing string

Preheat the oven to 190°C/375°F/gas5. Unroll the flap of meat attached to the loin. Slice halfway through the loin to make a pocket, leaving the ends of the loin uncut so the stuffing does not fall out during roasting. Season the pocket and cut side of the roast with salt, pepper and half the cinnamon. Trim 2 figs and cut them into quarters. Tuck these fig quarters into the pocket. Re-roll the roast and tie at regular intervals. Season with salt, pepper and the rest of the cinnamon.

Heat the butter and oil in a roasting pan until foaming. Add the pork and brown it on all sides. Pour over the stock and transfer to the oven. Roast, turning and basting the meat occasionally, until done, 1-1$^1/_4$ hours. If it gets dry, add more stock.

Meanwhile, glaze the figs: slice a cross-hatch in the top of each remaining fig and open it slightly like a flower. Pack the figs in a small baking dish, pour over half the port and sprinkle with the sugar. Bake in the oven with the pork until the figs are tender and glazed, 15-20 minutes. Remove them and keep warm.

When the roast is done, transfer it to a carving board and cover with foil. Add the remaining port, jelly and lemon juice to the pan and bring to the boil, stirring to dissolve the pan juices. Strain into a small pan and skim off excess fat. Add the fig juices to make about 375 ml/12 fl oz; if necessary, add more stock. Bring to the boil and whisk in the cornflour paste so it thickens slightly. Adjust the seasoning.

Discard the trussing strings and carve the roast into 1-cm/$^3/_8$ -inch slices. Arrange the slices overlapping on a warmed platter and spoon over a little sauce. Set the figs around the sides of the platter and serve the remaining sauce separately.

Pork fillet with muscat wine and dried cranberries

Pork fillet can be tied with string to form medallions of meat, ideal for pan-frying to serve with this sweet-and-sour gravy and an accompaniment of celeriac, turnip or potato. Other dried fruits, such as cherries or apricots, can be substituted if dried cranberries are hard to find.

SERVES 4

**2 pork fillets (about 750 g/
 1 ½ pounds)**
1 teaspoon ground cinnamon
salt and pepper
15 g/½ oz butter
1 tablespoon oil
60 g/2 oz dried cranberries
**250 ml/8 fl oz sweet white
 muscat wine**
**250 ml/8 fl oz brown beef or
 veal stock**
1 tablespoon redcurrant jelly
squeeze of lemon juice

Trim any skin and fat from the fillets. Lay them head to tail and tie them together with 8 pieces of string at even intervals to make a cylinder. Cut between each piece of string to make 8 medallions about 4 cm/1 ½ inches thick. Season the medallions with cinnamon, salt and pepper.

Heat the butter and oil in a frying pan until foaming. Add the medallions and sauté them until brown, 3-5 minutes. Turn them over, lower the heat and leave until browned on the outside and just cooked to your taste, 5-7 minutes. Transfer them to a plate and keep warm.

Discard all but a teaspoon of fat from the pan. Add the dried cranberries, wine and stock and boil until reduced by half, stirring to dissolve pan juices, 10-12 minutes Add the redcurrant jelly and lemon juice and stir until dissolved. Taste and adjust the seasoning.

Add the medallions to the sauce in the pan and reheat for 1 minute. Discard the strings, arrange the medallions on 4 warmed individual plates and spoon over the sauce.

Braised ham in apple juice with ginger-stuffed apples

To cook ham with apple is a tradition in Normandy, where pigs are often raised beneath the apple trees. Use mildly cured ham and apples on the tart side for this braise.

SERVES 6-8

**1 uncooked ham
(1.4 kg/3 pounds)
1 tablespoon vegetable oil
15 g/½ oz butter
2 carrots, sliced
2 onions, chopped
1 celery stalk, sliced
1 teaspoon whole cloves
750 ml/1¼ pints apple juice,
more if needed
1 tablespoon cornflour mixed
to a paste with 3 tablespoons
of the apple juice
pepper**

FOR THE GINGER-STUFFED
APPLES

**6-8 small tart apples
(about 1.15 kg/2½ pounds),
preferably Granny Smith
60 g/2 oz butter
60 g/2 oz dark brown sugar
30 g/1 oz raisins
2 tablespoons chopped
preserved ginger
½ teaspoon ground nutmeg
75 ml/2½ fl oz apple juice**

Preheat the oven to 160°C/325°F/gas3. Heat the oil and butter in a large flameproof casserole. Add the carrots, onions, celery and cloves and sauté until soft, stirring occasionally, 5-7 minutes.

Trim away any skin and all but a thin layer of fat from ham. Score the fat in a lattice pattern. Set the ham on top of vegetables, pour over the apple juice and bring to the boil. Cover, transfer to the preheated oven and braise until the ham is done, 1-1¼ hours. Baste the ham often and if the casserole gets dry during braising, add more juice.

Meanwhile, prepare the apples: cut them in halves at their equators and scoop out the cores. Trim the stem and flower ends, but do not peel. Put the apples cut side up in a shallow baking dish. In a mixing bowl, cream the butter and beat the sugar into it until soft and light. Stir in the raisins, ginger and nutmeg. Spoon the mixture into the apple cavities. Pour the apple juice into the baking dish and bake in the oven with the ham, basting occasionally, until the apples are very tender, 40-50 minutes. Transfer to a dish and cover with foil to keep warm. Reserve the juices in the baking dish.

When the ham is done, transfer to a cutting board. Cover to keep warm. Strain the cooking juices into a pan and skim off the fat. Stir in the juices from the baked apples – there should be about 375 ml/12 fl oz in total. If necessary, boil them until reduced. Whisk enough cornflour paste into the boiling juices to thicken the sauce until it lightly coats the back of a spoon. Taste and adjust the seasoning.

Carve the ham and arrange the slices on a warmed platter, or carve it at the table. Arrange the baked apples around the ham. Moisten both with a little sauce and serve the rest separately.

Scandinavian meat dumplings with mushroom sauce *Frikadeller*

Frikadeller are often served as a main course with boiled potatoes and pickled beetroots, or you can add them to soup, cooking the dumplings in the broth.

SERVES 4-6

375 g/³⁄₄ pound veal, minced
375 g/³⁄₄ pound pork, minced
2 slices of white bread
250 ml/8 fl oz milk
I small onion, grated
2 egg yolks
¼ teaspoon grated nutmeg
¼ teaspoon allspice
salt and pepper
I litre/1²⁄₃ pints veal or chicken
   stock
125 ml/4 fl oz white wine
125 ml/4 fl oz white wine
   vinegar or cider vinegar

FOR THE MUSHROOM SAUCE

75 g/2½ oz butter
30 g/1 oz flour
375 g/³⁄₄ pound mushrooms,
   thinly sliced
2 shallots, finely chopped
I garlic clove, finely chopped
2 tablespoons chopped parsley

Pull the bread into pieces and soak it in the milk. In a bowl, combine the veal, pork, onion, egg yolks, nutmeg, allspice, salt and pepper, and beat with a wooden spoon to mix. Squeeze excess liquid from the soaked bread, pull it apart into crumbs and add to the meat mixture. Beat until smooth, adding a little milk if the mixture is dry.

Bring a small pan of water to the boil and poach 1 teaspoon of the seasoned mixture. Taste and adjust the seasoning of the remaining mixture, if necessary – it should be quite highly seasoned. Shape the mixture into walnut-sized meatballs.

Bring the stock, white wine and vinegar to the boil. Add half the meatballs and simmer until done, 8-10 minutes. With a draining spoon, transfer them to a baking dish, cover with foil and keep warm in a low oven. Simmer the remaining meatballs and drain. Boil the stock until reduced by half and set this aside for the sauce.

Make the mushroom sauce: in a small bowl, work half the butter with the flour to a paste with a fork; set aside. Melt the remaining butter in a frying pan, add the mushrooms and sauté, stirring occasionally, until tender, 2-3 minutes. Add the shallots, garlic, salt and pepper and sauté until the mushrooms are browned and the shallots are tender, 1-2 minutes. Stir in the reserved reduced stock and simmer 5 minutes. Whisk the flour and butter paste into the simmering sauce, a few pieces at a time, whisking constantly so the sauce thickens evenly. It should lightly coat the back of a spoon; if it is thin, continue simmering to reduce it.

Stir in the chopped parsley, taste the sauce and adjust the seasoning if necessary. Add the simmered meatballs to the hot sauce and heat gently so the flavours blend, 3-5 minutes. Taste the sauce again and adjust the seasoning, if necessary.

Prosciutto with rocket and grapefruit in balsamic vinaigrette

Balsamic vinegar suits fruit, its mellowed flavour pairing particularly well with fresh citrus. Feel free to use olive or vegetable oil, as you prefer.

SERVES 4

3 pink grapefruits

125 g/4 oz thinly sliced prosciutto

large bunch of rocket (about 175 g/6 oz)

FOR THE BALSAMIC VINAIGRETTE

3 tablespoons balsamic vinegar

2 teaspoons Dijon-style mustard

salt and freshly ground black pepper

125 ml/4 fl oz olive or vegetable oil

Pare the zest from one of the grapefruits and cut this zest into julienne strips. Bring a small saucepan of water to the boil, add the strips of zest, simmer for 2 minutes and drain.

Slice off the top and bottom of each grapefruit, then cut away the zest, pith and skin, following the curve of the fruit. Cut the grapefruit segments from the membranes.

Make the vinaigrette. combine the vinegar, mustard, salt and pepper in a mixing bowl and whisk until smooth. Gradually whisk in the oil so the vinaigrette emulsifies and thickens slightly. Taste and adjust the seasoning.

Toss the rocket with about a third of the vinaigrette. Taste and adjust the seasoning again. Make a bed of greens on 4 individual plates. Arrange the grapefruit sections and slices of prosciutto, curled into roses, on top of the rocket. Spoon over the remaining dressing and sprinkle the salad with grapefruit julienne.

Braised venison with juniper and cream

This braise can be made with other game, including wild boar. Choose tougher cuts such as those from the leg, which benefit from slow cooking in moist heat. Cooking time varies with the age of the animal.

SERVES 4

**1-kg/2-pound piece of boneless
    leg of venison**

15 g/$\frac{1}{2}$ oz butter

3 tablespoons vegetable oil

2 tablespoons flour

salt and pepper

**250 ml/8 fl oz crème fraîche
    or double cream**

FOR THE MARINADE

**1 bottle (750 ml/1 $\frac{1}{4}$ pints) red
    wine**

2 onions, quartered

4 shallots, halved

3 garlic cloves, finely chopped

**1 leek, trimmed, split and
    thinly sliced**

2 carrots, sliced

**1 tablespoon juniper berries,
    crushed**

2 tablespoons vegetable oil

Make the marinade: combine the wine, onions, shallots, garlic, leek, carrots and juniper berries in a saucepan. Bring to the boil and simmer 10 minutes. Leave the marinade to cool.

Tie the meat at regular intervals. Put the meat and marinade in a deep non-metallic bowl and spoon over the oil. Cover and leave to marinate in the refrigerator, stirring occasionally, for 1-2 days.

Preheat the oven to 160°C/325°F/gas3. Drain the meat and vegetables, reserving the marinade. Pat the meat dry with paper towels. Heat the butter and 2 tablespoons of the oil in a sauté pan or large flameproof casserole. Brown the venison over high heat on all sides, 5-7 minutes. Transfer the meat to a plate.

Add the remaining oil with the drained vegetables and flavourings from the marinade to the casserole and sauté until lightly browned, 4-6 minutes. Sprinkle over the flour and cook, stirring, until browned, 1-2 minutes. Return the venison to the casserole and stir in the marinade, salt and pepper – the meat should be completely covered. Cover with a lid and bring to the boil. Transfer to the preheated oven and cook, stirring occasionally, until meat is done, 2-3 hours. If the casserole gets dry during cooking, add a little water.

Transfer the venison to a platter and cover with foil to keep it warm. Strain the cooking juices into a saucepan, pressing down on the vegetables to extract all the liquid. Skim off any fat and boil, stirring often, to reduce and concentrate the flavour, 5-10 minutes – the sauce should be thick enough to coat the back of a spoon. Stir in the cream and bring just back to the boil. Taste and adjust the seasoning. Discard the trussing strings from the venison, cut it into slices, moisten them with some sauce and serve the remaining sauce separately.

Country terrine with hazelnuts   *Pâté de campagne aux noisettes*

Make this classic French terrine at least 3 days – and up to a week – ahead so the flavours have time to mellow and blend. Fat bacon can be substituted for barding fat.

SERVES 6-8

250 g/½ pound lean pork,
   minced
250 g/½ pound fat pork,
   minced
250 g/½ pound veal, minced
250 g/½ pound chicken livers,
   minced
250 g/½ pound barding fat
15 g/½ oz butter
1 onion, chopped
2 garlic cloves, finely chopped
¾ teaspoon ground allspice
pinch of ground cloves
pinch of grated nutmeg
2 eggs, beaten to mix
2 tablespoons brandy
1 teaspoon salt, more if needed
¾ teaspoon pepper
45 g/1½ oz hazelnuts, toasted
   and skinned
1 bay leaf
sprig of thyme

1.5-litre/2⅓- pint terrine mould

Line the bottom and sides of the mould with barding fat, reserving some of it for the top. Preheat the oven to 175°C/350°F/gas4. Half-fill a roasting pan with water for a water bath.

Melt the butter in a pan and sauté the onion until soft but not brown. In a bowl, combine the onion, lean and fat pork, veal, chicken livers, garlic, spices, eggs, brandy, salt and pepper. Beat with a wooden spoon to mix the flavourings thoroughly. Stir in the hazelnuts. Melt some butter in a pan and sauté a small piece of the mixture. Taste and adjust the seasoning of remaining mixture if necessary – it should be highly seasoned. Continue beating the mixture until it holds together, pulling away from sides of bowl, 2-3 minutes.

Pack the mixture into the lined mould, smooth the top and cover with the remaining barding fat. Set the bay leaf and thyme on top. Cover the terrine with a lid, set in the water bath and bring the water to the boil on the hob. Transfer to the preheated oven and bake until done, 1¼ -1½ hours. If the water in the bath evaporates, add more.

When the terrine is cooked, remove from the water bath and leave until tepid. Remove the cover and set a 1-kg/2-pound weight on top so that the terrine is compressed and firm for slicing. Store the weighted terrine in the refrigerator.

Discard the bay leaf and thyme. Serve from the mould or turn it out and cut it into 1-cm/⅜-inch slices.

Vegetables

Learning how to get the best out of vegetables is inherently very straightforward, but the challenge lies in the sheer diversity of the vegetable kingdom: be they leaves, roots, shoots, stems, stalks, fruits or even flowers. For example, the glorious artichoke is indeed a thistle bud and, after cooking, you can spread back the leaves and scoop out the monster of a choke to leave space for a filling of fresh tomato and goats' cheese, or a Provençal mixture of ground pork, garlic, wild thyme, olives and breadcrumbs. Asparagus, on the other hand, is a simple stalk I really prefer served with only a coating of melted butter or a vinaigrette.

Favourite recipes of mine for greens include dandelion leaves in hot bacon dressing, green cabbage

stuffed with pork and chestnuts, and the amazing *gumbo z'herbes* from Louisiana which includes at least seven different greens, plus okra to give it body. There are wonderful Oriental ways of cooking greens, too, like Chinese stir-fried spinach with charred garlic, and Indian braised greens with paneer cheese.

Even humble roots can be magnificent. A dish of scalloped potatoes baked in milk is the simplest of gratins; with onion, veal stock and Gruyère cheese, a gratin becomes *savoyarde*, while *gratin dauphinois* baked with cream and topped with cheese is perhaps the most famous of all. Think of dishes like roasted winter roots with a topping of chopped walnuts, or Jerusalem artichokes stewed with ham and tomato in white wine; or Chinese carnelian carrots with star anise, ginger, sugar, soy sauce and rice wine.

Roasted tomato, mushroom, onion and garlic bruschetta

These vegetables, particularly the cherry tomatoes, fare very well in the high heat of an oven set for roasting, where flavours concentrate and sweeten. If you add tougher vegetables, such as fennel, cut them into small pieces so they roast as quickly as the more tender ones. The rest is simple!

SERVES 4 AS A STARTER

500 g/1 pound cherry tomatoes

2 onions

8 garlic cloves

125 g/4 oz chestnut or other brown mushrooms

3 tablespoons olive oil, more if needed

salt and freshly ground black pepper

8 small slices of Italian bread, cut 2 cm/³⁄₄ inch thick

1 tablespoon balsamic vinegar

1 tablespoon coarsely chopped flat-leaf parsley

2-3 tablespoons coarsely chopped basil

Remove the stems from tomatoes. Peel the onions, keeping the roots intact, and cut them in half, through root and stem. Thinly slice each half into crescents. Peel the garlic cloves and halve them lengthwise. Trim the mushroom stems and halve the mushrooms if small or quarter them if large.

Preheat the oven to 260°C/500°F/gas10 or its highest possible setting. Toss the tomatoes, onion, garlic and mushrooms with 1 tablespoon of the olive oil and some salt and pepper. Spread them in a pan just big enough to hold the vegetables in a single layer. Roast them in the preheated oven until tender and browned, stirring once, 6-8 minutes. When done, toss the vegetables with the vinegar and chopped herbs. Taste, adjust seasoning and keep warm.

Meanwhile, toast the bread: brush both sides of the bread slices with the remaining olive oil. Lay them directly on an oven rack and toast in the preheated oven until golden, turning once, 6-8 minutes. Top the slices of bread with the roasted vegetables and serve at once.

Asparagus in puff pastry *Feuilletés aux asperges*

This classic French marriage of asparagus and puff pastry is ideal for spring when asparagus is in season.

SERVES 6

1 kg/2 lb green or white asparagus
1 kg/2 lb puff pastry (page 168)
1 egg mixed with ½ teaspoon salt for the glaze

FOR THE TARRAGON BUTTER SAUCE
juice of ½ lemon, or to taste
250 g/8 oz butter, cold and cut into pieces
3 tablespoons chopped tarragon
salt and white pepper

On a floured surface, roll the pastry to a 52x25-cm/21x10-inch rectangle and trim the edges. Halve lengthwise into 2 long strips and cut at an angle to make 3 diamond shapes. Turn over and place on a baking sheet sprinkled with water. Press down lightly and brush with egg. Slash each in a lattice pattern with the a knife point and chill until firm, 15-30 minutes. Preheat the oven to 240°C/475°F/gas9.

Bake pastries until starting to brown, 5 minutes, then lower heat to 200°C/400°F/gas6 and bake until done, 15-20 minutes. Split each in half horizontally and keep warm.

Make the sauce: in a heavy pan, heat 30g/1oz butter with the lemon juice, whisking, until it softens. Whisk in the rest of the butter, a little at a time, working on and off the heat so it thickens the sauce without melting to oil. Whisk in the tarragon and season.

Place the pastry 'bottoms' on warmed plates and arrange the asparagus on them. Spoon over the sauce, cover with the pastry 'lids', slightly askew, and serve at once.

Broccoli and cauliflower with lemon butter sauce

A bright lemon butter sauce dresses up these everyday vegetables, which make cheerful accompaniments to poultry and all sorts of fish. Using the baby cauliflowers now becoming so readily available can make this a very attractive dish.

SERVES 3-4

**1 head of broccoli
(about 500 g/1 pound)
½ head of cauliflower (about
375 g/¾ pound)**

FOR THE LEMON BUTTER SAUCE
**175 g/6 oz butter, cold and cut
into pieces
2 shallots, chopped
1 tablespoon double cream
juice of 1 lemon, more if
needed
salt and white pepper**

Trim the broccoli and cauliflower and cut them into large florets, discarding the stems. Rinse and drain them separately. Bring 2 large pans of salted water to the boil. Add the cauliflower to one pan and the broccoli to the other and simmer, uncovered, until done, 5-7 minutes for the broccoli and 7-10 minutes for the cauliflower.

Meanwhile, make the sauce: in a medium saucepan, melt 30 g/1 oz of the butter, add the shallots and sauté them until soft but not browned, 1-2 minutes. Stir in the double cream and simmer until the liquid is reduced by about half, 1-2 minutes.

Whisk in the remaining butter, a little at a time, working on and off the heat so it thickens the sauce without melting to oil. Whisk in the lemon juice, taste and adjust the seasoning. Keep warm on a rack set over a pan of warm (not hot) water.

Thoroughly drain the cooked broccoli and cauliflower and arrange in a pattern of alternating colours on a warmed serving. Pour over the sauce and serve at once.

My mother's pea soup

When I was a child, in early June I would be put to shelling peas. Some were plump and some were skinny, so my mother would solve the problem of cooking them all evenly by simmering them in a soup, flavouring it lavishly with fresh mint.

SERVES 4-6

1.15 kg/2½ pounds fresh peas
30 g/1 oz butter
1 onion, finely chopped
1 garlic clove, finely chopped
1 litre/1⅔ pints chicken stock
1 teaspoon sugar
salt and white pepper
large bunch of fresh mint
125 ml/4 fl oz double cream,
   plus more for serving
   (optional)

Shell the peas: there should be about 500 g/1 pound. Melt the butter in a large pan, add the onion and garlic and cook until soft but not brown, 3-4 minutes. Add the peas, stock, sugar, salt and pepper. Cover and bring to the boil. Reduce the heat and simmer until done, 10-15 minutes, depending on the maturity of the peas.

Strip the mint leaves from the stems, reserving 4 sprigs for garnish. Chop the leaves. With a slotted spoon, remove the peas, onion and garlic from the stock. Purée them in a food processor with a little of the cooking liquid until smooth. Work the purée through a sieve into a large pan, strain in the cooking liquid and stir the soup until well blended.

To finish: bring the soup to the boil, stir in the cream and chopped mint. Adjust the seasoning. Ladle into 4 warmed bowls. If you like, add a spoonful of double cream to each bowl and stir to marble it. Top with mint sprigs and serve at once.

Cream of corn chowder

Chowder made with freshly picked corn is astonishingly sweet and rich. In the USA, where the soup originates, special hexagonal chowder crackers are sold to soak in the soup and give it body. Crumbled water biscuits are a good alternative.

SERVES 4-6

6 ears of fresh corn

1 litre/1$\frac{2}{3}$ pints milk

salt and white pepper

45 g/1$\frac{1}{2}$ oz butter

1 onion, chopped

1$\frac{1}{2}$ tablespoons flour

250 ml/8 fl oz double cream

large pinch of freshly grated nutmeg

3-4 tablespoons chopped fresh chives

Strip the hulls and silk from the ears of corn. Holding an ear upright on a chopping board, cut off the kernels with a sharp knife, working from top to bottom and rotating the ear until all the kernels are removed. Repeat with the remaining ears and put the kernels in a medium saucepan. Add about a quarter of the milk with salt and pepper. Simmer the corn until tender, 7-10 minutes. Purée it in a food processor, or work it through a food mill.

Wipe out the pan and melt the butter in it. Add the onion and sauté until it is translucent and tender but not starting to brown. Stir in the flour and cook for 30 seconds. Whisk in the remaining milk and bring the mixture to the boil, whisking constantly until it thickens lightly. Stir in the corn purée, cream, nutmeg and more salt and pepper, and bring the chowder almost back to the boil. Taste and adjust the seasoning.

The chowder can be refrigerated for a day and reheated just before serving. Serve it in warmed bowls, sprinkled with chopped chives.

Artichokes with sauce gribiche

This light version of mayonnaise, called sauce gribiche, is excellent with many cold cooked vegetables such as asparagus, broccoli or cauliflower. Here I suggest serving it with large artichokes, and it is also good with little ones, so small they contain no choke and are totally edible. Trim the tips of the leaves of little artichokes and peel the stem, as you can eat much of its centre. As this recipe uses raw egg, remember the potential risk of salmonella, especially to vulnerable people.

SERVES 4

4 large globe artichokes
½ lemon
4 garlic cloves

FOR THE GRIBICHE SAUCE

2 hard-boiled eggs
1 raw egg yolk
salt and pepper
250 ml/8 fl oz vegetable oil
2 tablespoons white wine
1 teaspoon Dijon-style mustard
1 tablespoon chopped gherkins
1 tablespoon capers, rinsed and
   drained
2 tablespoons chopped parsley
juice of ½ lemon

Bring a large pan of salted water to the boil. Break off the stem from each artichoke so that any fibres are pulled out. Trim the bases with a knife so they sit flat and rub the cut surfaces with lemon to prevent discoloration. Add the lemon half to the pan. Trim the leaves with scissors to remove spines. With a large knife, cut off the pointed top of the artichoke, parallel to the base. Push a garlic clove into the leaves of each artichoke. Add them to the boiling water and lay a heavy heatproof plate on top to keep them submerged. Simmer uncovered until done, 30-50 minutes, depending on age and size. Drain the artichokes upside down, so no water is trapped by the leaves. Let cool.

Make the gribiche sauce: separate the hard-boiled egg whites from the yolks, coarsely chop the whites and set aside. Force the cooked yolks through a sieve into a bowl. Mix in the raw egg yolk with a large pinch of salt. Whisk in about 2 tablespoons of oil, very slowly at first, until the mixture thickens, as for mayonnaise. Whisk in the white wine. Continue whisking in the remaining oil in a slow steady stream. Stir in the mustard, reserved egg whites, gherkins, capers, parsley and lemon juice. Taste and adjust the seasoning.

To finish the artichokes: grasp the central cone of leaves and lift out with a quick twist. Reserve it, discarding the garlic. With a teaspoon, carefully scoop out the fibrous choke and discard it. Set the cones of leaves upside down in the centre of each artichoke. Place the artichokes on individual plates and spoon some sauce into each cup of leaves. Serve the rest separately.

Gratin of leeks and ham

When we lived in Paris, this gratin was a favourite supper dish, the complex flavours of the béchamel marrying plain leeks and ham to unexpected harmony. Braised chicory is an alternative to the leeks.

SERVES 6-8 AS A STARTER, OR
   4 AS A MAIN COURSE

4 medium leeks
   (about 1.25 kg/2$\frac{1}{2}$ pounds)
8-10 thin slices of cooked ham
   (about 375 g/$\frac{3}{4}$ pound)

FOR THE BÉCHAMEL SAUCE
500 ml/16 fl oz milk
1 large slice of onion
1 bay leaf
1/2 teaspoon peppercorns
45 g/1$\frac{1}{2}$ oz butter
3 tablespoons flour
salt and white pepper
generous pinch of freshly
   grated nutmeg

Preheat the oven to 175°C/350°F/gas4 and butter a medium gratin dish. Bring a large pan of salted water to the boil. Trim the leeks, discarding the roots and tough tops. Slit the trimmed leeks lengthwise, leaving them attached at root end, and wash thoroughly under cold running water. Tie the leeks together with string so they hold their shape in cooking. Add the leeks to the boiling water and simmer, uncovered, until tender, 10-15 minutes depending on their size.

Meanwhile, make the béchamel sauce: scald the milk with the onion, bay leaf and peppercorns. Cover and leave to infuse off the heat for 10-15 minutes. In a heavy-based saucepan, melt the butter, whisk in the flour and cook, stirring, until the flour is foaming but not browned, about 1 minute. Off the heat, strain in the hot milk. Whisk well, then bring to the boil, whisking constantly until the sauce thickens. Season to taste with salt, pepper and nutmeg and leave to simmer 1-2 minutes. Take off the heat, cover and set aside.

Drain the leeks, rinse with cold water and drain again thoroughly, squeezing them in your fists to extract any water. Cut the leeks into 8-10 pieces about 10 cm/4 inches long. Strip off 2-3 outer green leaves from one of the leeks. Lay these flat, slice them lengthwise into julienne strips and set aside for garnish.

Roll each leek section in a slice of ham and pack tightly in the buttered gratin dish. Spoon béchamel sauce on top and bake in the preheated oven until bubbling, 20-25 minutes. If not browned on top, grill 2-3 minutes until golden. Sprinkle the leek julienne on top and serve at once.

Lettuce packages au jus

When the first excitement of baby spring lettuce leads to endless quantities of tougher autumn greens, I start cooking. I long ago discovered these lettuce leaf packages as a pretty way to bundle braised lettuce. Serve them as a garnish for roast chicken or fish.

SERVES 4

**1 kg/2 lb cos or
butterhead lettuce
6 slices of bacon
(about 125 g/4 oz), diced
500 ml/16 fl oz chicken
or vegetable stock
salt and pepper
30 g/1 oz butter, cold and cut
into pieces**

Trim the lettuce stems and discard any wilted outer leaves. Select 8-12 perfect leaves, wash and dry them. Shred the remaining leaves, put them in a colander and rinse under cold water.

Bring a large pan of salted water to the boil. Add the whole lettuce leaves and blanch them for about 1 minute. Transfer the leaves to a bowl of cold water, then spread them out on paper towels, stem sides down. Leave to drain.

Fry the bacon in a sauté or deep frying pan until browned. Pour off excess fat, add the stock and bring to the boil, stirring to deglaze the pan juices. Stir in the shredded lettuce and simmer until wilted, 2-3 minutes.

Remove the lettuce and bacon with a slotted spoon and transfer to a large bowl. Strain the cooking liquid into a small saucepan and boil until reduced by half. Meanwhile, taste the lettuce mixture and adjust the seasoning. Place a spoonful of lettuce mixture in the centre of each blanched lettuce leaf. Fold the cut end up and over the filling, then fold in each side and roll into a package. Set the packages on a warmed serving dish, cover and keep warm.

Make the jus: whisk the butter into the reduced cooking liquid a few pieces at a time, working on and off the heat so the butter softens and thickens the jus without melting to oil. Taste the jus and adjust the seasoning, spoon over the lettuce packages and serve at once.

Sautéed peppery greens

Kale is a leafy member of the cabbage family with quite a peppery bite. If the leaves are very young and tender, they can be tossed in salads. More often, however, they need to be cooked – making a perfect side dish for grilled meats or roasted chicken. Other winter greens, like collard, turnip, chard, mustard – even Savoy cabbage or curly endive – do well too.

SERVES 4

500 g/1 pound kale
1 tablespoon vegetable oil
250 g/½ pound spicy Italian sausage meat
1 onion, chopped
3 garlic cloves, finely chopped
½ teaspoon red pepper flakes, or more to taste
salt and pepper

Wash the kale well, discarding tough stems. Drain and shake off as much water as possible from the leaves. Heat the oil in a frying pan, add the sausage meat and sauté, stirring, until browned, 3-5 minutes.

Stir the onion and garlic into the pan and sauté with the sausage meat until lightly browned and fragrant, 4-5 minutes.

Stir in the kale with a little salt and pepper and cook over high heat until wilted, 2-3 minutes. Lower the heat, cover the pan and leave to sweat until the kale is done, 10-12 minutes. Sprinkle with red pepper flakes, taste and adjust the seasoning. Serve at once.

Aubergine stacks with three cheeses

Aubergine slices replace bread in this 'sandwich' of ricotta and soft, creamy fresh goats' cheese, baked in tomato sauce and sprinkled with Parmesan.

SERVES 4

500 g/1 pound aubergine
salt and pepper
60 ml/2 fl oz olive oil
small bunch of basil
small bunch of parsley
250 g/½ pound ricotta cheese
175 g/6 oz soft fresh goats'
cheese
30 g/1 oz grated Parmesan
cheese

FOR THE TOMATO, GARLIC AND
OREGANO SAUCE

75 ml/2½ fl oz olive oil
3 onions, chopped
5 garlic cloves, finely chopped
1.5 kg/3 lb tomatoes, peeled,
seeded and chopped
90 ml/3 fl oz tomato purée
3-4 tablespoons chopped
oregano
pinch of sugar

4 individual gratin dishes

Preheat the oven to 190°C/375°F/gas5. Trim the aubergines and cut them across in sixteen 1.25-cm/½ -inch slices. Lay the slices in a single layer on a tray. Sprinkle generously with salt on both sides and leave for 20-30 minutes to draw out excess juices.

Rinse the aubergine, drain in a colander and pat dry with paper towels. Arrange on oiled baking sheets and brush with olive oil. Bake until well browned and crisp but still soft inside, turning once, 25-30 minutes. Let cool.

Make the sauce: heat the oil in a large deep pan and fry the onions over medium heat until soft and lightly browned, 4-5 minutes. Add the garlic and cook until fragrant, 1 minute. Stir in the tomatoes, tomato purée, oregano, sugar, salt and pepper. Cover and cook gently until the tomatoes are very soft, 10-15 minutes. Uncover and continue cooking the sauce, stirring occasionally, until slightly thickened but still falling easily from the spoon, 5-10 minutes. Adjust the seasoning.

Strip the leaves from the herb stems and chop them. Beat the ricotta and goats' cheeses in a bowl until smooth. Stir in the chopped herbs and season. Brush the gratin dishes with olive oil and place an aubergine slice in each. Spread 2 tablespoons of cheese mixture on each slice and top with a second. Repeat with remaining filling and slices to make 4-layer stacks. Spoon over the sauce and sprinkle with Parmesan. Bake until very hot and bubbling, 20-25 minutes.

Pat's stuffed courgettes

Ask a New Englander for a recipe for squash and you'll get a winner. Bostonian Pat Kelly has had much experience dealing with the annual glut of courgettes and yellow squash, and suggests this simple recipe, equally good as an accompaniment to fish, meat or poultry.

SERVES 4

750 g/1½ pounds small courgettes or yellow squash
2 slices of white bread
60 g/2 oz butter, melted
1 medium onion, chopped
2 garlic cloves, chopped
1 medium tomato, peeled, seeded and chopped
45 g/1½ oz grated Gruyère cheese
3-4 tablespoons chopped thyme
grated zest of 1 lemon
½ teaspoon freshly grated nutmeg
salt and pepper

Preheat the oven to 175°C/350°F/gas4. Bring a large pan of salted water to the boil. Trim the ends of the courgettes or squash and cut in half lengthwise. Scoop out the seeds with a teaspoon. Add the vegetables to the boiling water and blanch for 8-10 minutes. Drain, rinse with cold water and leave to drain thoroughly.

For the stuffing, tear the bread into pieces and work to crumbs in a food processor. Heat half the butter in a frying pan, add the onion and sauté until soft but not brown, 3-5 minutes. Stir in the garlic and continue cooking for 1 minute. Let cool slightly, then stir in the breadcrumbs, chopped tomato, grated cheese, thyme, lemon zest, nutmeg, salt and pepper. Taste and adjust the seasoning.

Fill this stuffing into the courgettes or squash, mounding it well. Set them in a buttered baking dish and moisten with the remaining butter. Bake in the preheated oven until done and the top is browned, 20-25 minutes.

PAT'S PRAWN-STUFFED COURGETTES

For a more substantial dish, add about 125 g/4 oz chopped cooked peeled prawns to the stuffing.

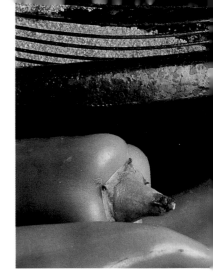

Mexican stuffed peppers

Chiles rellenos

Classic *chiles rellenos* are stuffed with cheese then dipped in batter and fried, but when properly done they are not at all heavy. Anaheim peppers can be quite hot, so I suggest a mild, cooling salsa.

SERVES 4

125-g/4-oz piece of Monterey Jack (or sharp Cheddar) cheese

8 Anaheim or New Mexico chilli peppers (about 625 g/1 ¼ pounds), with stems attached

150 g/5 oz fine yellow cornmeal, more if needed

3 eggs, separated

salt and pepper

vegetable oil for frying

FOR THE TOMATO AND CORIANDER SALSA

500 g/1 pound tomatoes, peeled, seeded and chopped

2 garlic cloves, finely chopped

1 large onion, chopped

1 green or red sweet pepper, seeded and chopped

small bunch of coriander, leaves chopped

juice of 1 lemon

Make the salsa: mix together the tomatoes, garlic, onion, sweet pepper and coriander in a non-metallic bowl. Stir in the lemon juice and season to taste. Let stand at room temperature for at least 30 minutes.

Preheat the grill. Cut the cheese into sticks just shorter than the length of the peppers. Rub the peppers with oil and roast over an open flame or under the grill, turning them until the skin chars and bursts, 10-12 minutes. Put them in a plastic bag to retain steam, as this will help loosen the skins. Leave them to cool.

Peel the peppers, keeping any stems attached. Carefully make a slit in the side of each, stopping short of the stem and pointed ends. With the tip of a knife or fingers, pull out the cores and seeds. Insert the cheese sticks into the peppers.

Spread the cornmeal on a plate. Beat the egg yolks with salt and pepper. Whip the egg whites with a pinch of salt until soft peaks form and fold these into the beaten yolks. Holding the peppers by the stems, dip them into the egg mixture. Roll the peppers in cornmeal to coat them.

Heat 6 mm/¼ inch oil in a cast-iron skillet or frying pan until hot but not smoking. Fry the peppers until golden brown on all sides, 3-5 minutes. Drain them on paper towels and serve at once, with the salsa in a separate bowl.

Mexican stuffed peppers

Warm potato salad with tarragon and white wine

Potatoes have more flavour when they are cooked in their skins and, when peeled while still warm, they absorb more dressing. Served warm, the salad is a classic accompaniment to hot garlic sausage, but also goes well with most barbecued or cold meat dishes. Flat-leaf parsley can be substituted for the tarragon.

SERVES 4

750 g/1½ lb waxy potatoes, scrubbed but unpeeled
60 ml/2 fl oz white wine
salt and freshly ground black pepper
bunch of tarragon
125 ml/4 fl oz olive oil

Put the potatoes in a large pan of cold salted water. Cover, bring to the boil, and simmer until done, 15-20 minutes. Drain.

When cool enough to handle, peel and cut into 2.5-cm/1-inch chunks. Sprinkle with the wine, season and stir gently. Leave to cool until tepid.

Meanwhile, strip the tarragon leaves from stems and coarsely chop the leaves. Sprinkle the tarragon and oil over the potatoes and toss gently to mix. Taste, adjust the seasoning and serve while still warm.

Indonesian salad with spicy peanut sauce *Gado gado*

A wide variety of vegetables in contrasting colours should be used for this Indonesian salad. They are usually blanched, but should remain crunchy. The tangy peanut dressing, *bumbu saté*, tastes better and better on standing.

SERVES 4-6

250 g/½ pound mange-tout peas, trimmed

125 g/¼ pound beansprouts

250 g/½ pound carrots, peeled and cut into julienne strips

175 g/6 oz green beans, trimmed

FOR THE SPICY PEANUT SAUCE

250 ml/8 fl oz crunchy peanut butter

½ onion, chopped

1 garlic clove

¼ teaspoon red pepper flakes, or more to taste

1 teaspoon ground ginger

½ teaspoon brown sugar

juice of ½ lime, plus more if needed

175 ml/6 fl oz hot water, plus more if needed

soy sauce

pepper

Make the spicy peanut sauce: in a blender or food processor, combine the peanut butter, onion, garlic, pepper flakes, ginger, sugar and lime juice. Purée until very smooth, adding hot water as necessary so the mixture churns well. Work in more hot water or lime juice, adding enough to make a sauce that is thick enough to coat the back of a spoon. Taste and adjust the seasoning with more lime juice, soy sauce and pepper. Set aside.

Bring a large pan of salted water to the boil. Add the mange-tout peas to the water and leave 30 seconds. Drain, refresh with cold water and drain again. Repeat the process for the beansprouts and carrots. Add the green beans to the boiling salted water and cook until perfectly blanched, 4-6 minutes. Drain, refresh with cold water and drain again.

Arrange the vegetables in individual mounds on a large serving platter. Serve the sauce separately in a bowl. The salad may be served at room temperature or chilled. Whisk in the remaining butter, a little at a time, working on and off the heat so it thickens the sauce without melting to oil.

Celeriac with piquant mayonnaise *Céleri rémoulade*

A *rémoulade* mayonnaise usually calls for the addition of capers, gherkin, anchovy and chopped herbs, but *céleri rémoulade* needs only mustard to highlight the distinctive bite of the celeriac.

SERVES 4-6

**1 celeriac root
(about 750 g/1 ½ lb)
1 lemon, halved**

FOR THE PIQUANT MAYONNAISE

**1 large or 2 small egg yolks
2 teaspoons Dijon-style mustard,
or to taste
2 tablespoons white wine vinegar
salt and white pepper
175 ml/6 fl oz vegetable oil**

Make the mayonnaise: in a small bowl, whisk the egg yolks with the mustard, half the vinegar and a little salt and pepper until slightly thickened, 1-2 minutes. Add the vegetable oil, drop by drop, whisking constantly. When 2 tablespoons of oil have been added, the mixture should be very thick. The remaining oil can be added a little more quickly, either 1 tablespoon at a time, beating thoroughly between each addition, or in a thin steady stream. When all the oil has been added, stir in the remaining vinegar. Taste the mayonnaise and adjust the seasoning – it should taste clearly of mustard.

Peel the celeriac and rub it with the cut lemon to prevent discoloration. Cut the root in julienne strips on a mandoline slicer or with a knife. Put the celeriac in a pan of cold salted water, bring to the boil and simmer for 1 minute. Drain, refresh and drain again. If the celeriac is fibrous, several minutes' blanching may be needed – it should be crisp but not tough.

Mix the mayonnaise thoroughly with the celeriac and season to taste with lemon juice, salt, pepper and more mustard if needed. Cover and refrigerate to allow the flavours to mellow for at least 1 hour and up to 12 hours.

Carrot purée with cardamom

Root vegetables have a natural affinity with warm, sweet spices like cardamom.

SERVES 4

**1 kg/2 pounds carrots, peeled
and thickly sliced
1 teaspoon cardamom pods
15 g/½ oz butter
½ teaspoon sugar
salt and pepper
60 ml/2 fl oz double cream,
more if needed**

Bring a large pan of salted water to the boil. Add the carrots, cover and simmer until they are very tender, 15-20 minutes.

Meanwhile, break open the cardamom pods and remove the seeds, discarding the shells. Crush the seeds in a mortar with a pestle or on a board under a heavy pan.

Drain the cooked carrots and purée in a food processor, or work through a sieve. Melt the butter in a pan. Add the purée and stir in the cardamom, sugar, salt and pepper. Beat in the cream. Heat, stirring, until very hot and thickened. If too thick, add more cream. Adjust the seasoning. Transfer to a warmed serving bowl.

Marinated mushrooms

Mushrooms can be marinated for just half an hour or up to a day. The longer they marinate, the moister they become, and the more the flavour intensifies.

SERVES 4

**500 g/1 pound small white
button mushrooms
3-4 tablespoons chopped fresh
chives**

FOR THE VINAIGRETTE
DRESSING
**1 tablespoon lemon juice
125 ml/4 fl oz olive oil
salt and pepper**

Wipe the mushrooms with a damp cloth and trim the stems level with the caps.

Make the vinaigrette dressing by whisking the ingredients together.

Put the mushrooms in a deep bowl, pour over the dressing and toss to coat. Cover and leave for 30 minutes or up to 2 hours at room temperature. (If marinating longer, store in the refrigerator and bring to room temperature before serving).

Stir the chopped chives into the mushrooms. Taste and adjust the seasoning. For cocktails, drain the mushrooms and spear them on toothpicks; as a first course, arrange them on the slices of toast, spooning over the marinade.

Root vegetable couscous

For luck, Moroccans add a combination of any seven vegetables to their couscous. Here I've used lots of roots, but cabbage, aubergine or leek can be substituted. Serve with Moroccan chilli paste (harissa), thinned with a little olive oil and lemon juice.

SERVES 8

500 g/1 pound new potatoes, peeled

500 g/1 pound parsnips, peeled

500 g/1 pound carrots, peeled

250 g/½ pound celeriac, peeled

250 g/½ pound butternut squash

bunch of coriander

bouquet garni

2 tablespoons olive oil

1 onion, chopped

1 teaspoon ground turmeric

1 teaspoon ground ginger

1 cinnamon stick, broken into pieces

1 kg/2 lb tomatoes, peeled, seeded and chopped

2 litres/3¼ pints chicken or vegetable stock, more if needed

salt and pepper

30 g/1 oz raisins

2-3 fresh red chilli peppers, cored, seeded and chopped

FOR THE COUSCOUS

50 g/1¾ oz flaked almonds

large pinch of saffron threads

625 g/1¼ pounds precooked couscous

45 g/1½ oz butter

1.5 litres/2⅓ pints boiling water

They key to success here is to cut the vegetables into larger or smaller chunks. depending on their toughness, so they all cook in the same time. Cut the potatoes into 2 or 3 pieces. Cut the parsnips and carrots at an angle into 2.5-cm/1-inch slices. Cut the celeriac into 8 wedges. Halve the squash lengthwise and scoop out the seeds. Lay flat side on a board and cut away the skin. Cut the flesh into 2.5-cm/1-inch chunks. Strip the coriander leaves from the stems. Chop and reserve the leaves; add the stems to the bouquet garni.

Heat the oil in a large pan and sauté the onion until soft but not brown, 3-4 minutes. Stir in the spices and sauté until fragrant, about 30 seconds. Stir in the tomatoes and cook, stirring, until softened, 4-5 minutes. Stir in the stock, root vegetables, bouquet garni, salt and pepper. Cover, bring to the boil and simmer, stirring occasionally, for 15-20 minutes. Stir in the squash, raisins, chillies and enough stock to cover. Continue simmering until very tender, 10-15 minutes. Discard the bouquet garni and cinnamon. Adjust the seasoning.

Meanwhile, prepare the couscous: preheat oven to 175°C/350°F/gas4. Spread almonds on a baking sheet and toast in the oven until lightly browned, stirring once, 12-15 minutes. Pour 2-3 tablespoons of the boiling water over the saffron and leave to infuse. Put the couscous and butter in a large bowl, pour over the remaining boiling water and add the saffron and its liquid (couscous may require more or less water, so follow pack instructions). Stir quickly with a fork and let stand until plump, about 5 minutes. Taste and adjust the seasoning.

Spoon into 8 warmed shallow bowls, making wells in the centre. With a slotted spoon, transfer the vegetables to the wells. Pour over the broth, and sprinkle with toasted almonds and chopped coriander to serve.

Japanese deep-fried vegetables *Vegetable tempura*

Here I suggest just three vegetables, but other possibilities include spring onion, aubergine, courgette and firm avocado. Serve with a soy dipping sauce.

SERVES 4-6

250 g/½ pound green asparagus
1 small aubergine (about 375 g/¾ pound)
250 g/½ pound shiitake mushrooms
oil for deep-frying
60 g/2 oz flour (for coating)

FOR THE TEMPURA BATTER

1 egg
250 ml/8 fl oz cold water
1 tablespoon groundnut oil
125 g/4 oz flour
1 teaspoon baking powder
1 teaspoon salt

Trim the asparagus and peel the stems. Peel the aubergine and cut into 6-mm/¼ -inch rounds. Wipe the mushrooms with a damp cloth, trim the stems level with the caps and cut any large ones in half. Dry the vegetables thoroughly before coating with flour.

Make the batter: beat the egg in a bowl just until mixed. Stir in the water and oil. Sift in the flour, baking powder and salt, and stir until just combined. The batter should remain lumpy or it will be heavy when fried.

In a wok or deep-fryer, heat the oil to 190°C/375°F. Toss the asparagus spears in flour to coat lightly, then dip in batter one by one so completely coated. Lift out and let excess batter drain. Lower into hot oil and deep-fry until done, 2-3 minutes, stirring gently with a draining spoon.

Drain on paper towels and keep warm, uncovered, in a low oven with the door open, while you fry the other vegetables. Arrange on a serving platter and serve at once, with a soy dipping sauce.

Caramelized onion quiche

Here an intense confit of onions cooked in red wine gives a contemporary twist to quiche. Serve it warm as a starter, or for lunch or brunch with a seasonal green salad.

SERVES 6-8

30 g / 1 oz butter

500 g/1 lb yellow onions, thinly sliced

salt and pepper

2-3 tablespoons sugar

75 ml/2½ fl oz red wine

1 tablespoon chopped thyme

FOR THE FRENCH PIE PASTRY

200 g/6½ oz flour

100 g/3¼ oz butter

1 egg yolk

1/2 teaspoon salt

3 tablespoons water, more if needed

FOR THE CUSTARD

3 eggs, plus 3 extra egg yolks

500 ml/16 fl oz milk

125 ml/4 fl oz double cream, or more milk

pinch of nutmeg

white pepper

25-cm/10-inch tart pan with removable base

Make the French pie pastry: sift the flour on to a work surface and make a well in the centre. Pound the butter with a rolling pin to soften it. Put the butter, egg yolk, salt and water into the well. With your fingers, work the moist ingredients until thoroughly mixed. Draw in the flour with a pastry scraper and work in the other ingredients with the fingers of both hands until coarse crumbs form. If the crumbs are very dry, add 1-2 tablespoons more water. Press the dough into a ball.

Lightly flour the work surface. Blend the dough by pushing it away from you with the heel of your hand, then gathering it up until it is very smooth and peels away from the work surface in one piece, 1-2 minutes. Shape into a ball, wrap and chill until firm, at least 30 minutes.

Meanwhile, make the confit: heat the butter in a frying pan and add the onions with some salt and pepper. Press a piece of buttered foil on top, cover and sweat the onions, stirring occasionally, until soft, 10-15 minutes. Sprinkle with the sugar, turn up the heat and cook until golden brown, 5-10 minutes. Stir in the wine and cook, stirring often, until the liquid has evaporated and onions are deep brown, 15-20 minutes. Stir the thyme into the confit, adjust the seasoning and let it cool.

Use the pastry to line the tart pan and chill until firm, about 15 minutes. Preheat the oven to 220°C/425°F/gas7 and blind-bake the pastry shell (lined with greaseproof paper and weighted with beans). Adjust the oven to 190°C/375°F/gas5.

Make the custard: in a bowl, whisk the eggs, egg yolks, milk, cream, nutmeg, salt and white pepper just until mixed. Spread the cooled onions evenly in the base of the pastry shell and pour over the custard. Bake in the oven until the custard is browned on top and just set, 30-35 minutes. Let cool slightly before unmoulding.

Serve the quiche warm or at room temperature.

Pasta, grains & pulses

Staples they may be, but these humble ingredients are capable of infinite variety. Pasta can be tossed simply with oil or butter and herbs, or with a sauce that dresses the strands – classics include *spaghetti alla carbonara* with pancetta, Parmesan and egg; *spaghetti alla puttanesca* with anchovies, capers, olives and tomatoes; and spaghettini with little clams, garlic, parsley and olive oil. Shaped pastas, particularly hollow ones such as penne or rigatoni, hold more sauce and invite coarser, more moist mixtures such as a traditional *ragù*. Shells suggest shellfish to me, and other shapes like snails, a rustic, earthy approach with lots of herbs and garlic. Other nations chip in with recipes like Thai rice noodles with beansprouts and long beans in a

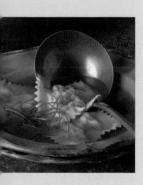

curry coconut sauce, or Alsatian saddle of hare with noodles and wild mushrooms in cream.

Boiled or steamed grains may be served plain, or tossed with herbs, spices or cooked vegetables such as sautéed onion and mushrooms.

Rice, by far the most common whole grain, turns up often in ethnic dishes such as stir-fried Indonesian rice with chicken, garlic, egg, hot red pepper; or Iranian crispy baked rice cake with saffron. Risottos can be showcases for all sorts of added ingredients, from peas and courgettes to braised meats; while pilafs lend themselves to spices such as cardamom, cumin and saffron, particularly with white rice. The way is also open to more substantial additions like the ham, prawns and tomato of American jambalaya, or the lamb, tomato and onion of Russian *plov*.

Spaghetti with bacon, tomatoes and chilli *Spaghetti all'amatriciana*

This is a great dish for those evenings when time and energy are short. Tomatoes are the focus, so be sure they are perfectly ripe – as a time saver, you'll find that plum tomatoes really do not need to be peeled.

SERVES 4-6

500 g/1 pound spaghetti

**8 slices of bacon
(about 175 g/6 oz), diced**

1 onion, thinly sliced

125 ml/4 fl oz dry white wine

**1 kg/2 pounds tomatoes,
peeled, seeded and chopped**

**¼ teaspoon red chilli pepper
flakes,**

more to taste

salt and pepper

**75 g/2½ oz grated Parmesan
cheese**

Heat a large frying pan. Add the bacon and cook until the fat runs and the bacon starts to brown, 3-5 minutes. Add the onion and sauté until soft and lightly browned, 4-5 minutes.

Add the wine and boil until reduced by half. Stir in the tomatoes and red pepper flakes, bring to the boil and simmer until the sauce is thickened, 12-15 minutes. Taste and adjust the seasoning.

Meanwhile, bring a large pan of salted water to the boil. Add the spaghetti and stir to separate the strands. Simmer until al dente, tender but still firm to the bite, 7-10 minutes. Drain, return to the pan and add the tomato sauce and half the Parmesan cheese. Toss until the spaghetti is thoroughly coated with sauce. Taste, adjust the seasoning and transfer to warmed individual bowls. Serve at once, with remaining grated Parmesan cheese in a separate bowl.

SPAGHETTI WITH OLIVES, TOMATOES AND CHILLI

For a vegetarian version of this spaghetti, omit the bacon and fry the onion in 2 tablespoons olive oil. Add 60 g/2 oz black olives to the sauce with the red pepper flakes, stoning the olives first if you like.

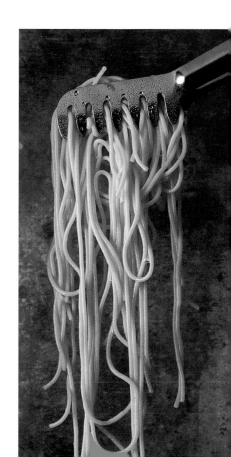

Spaghetti with red mussel sauce

**The fewer the ingredients, the better they must
be – the freshest of mussels and the ripest of
tomatoes are important here.**

SERVES 4

500 g/1 pound spaghetti
60 ml/2 fl oz olive oil
salt and pepper
2 tablespoons chopped parsley

FOR THE RED MUSSEL SAUCE

1.8 kg/4 pounds small mussels
2 tablespoons olive oil
2 onions, finely chopped
6 garlic cloves, finely chopped
1.4 kg/3 pounds tomatoes,
**   peeled, seeded and chopped**
1 bay leaf

Bring a large pan of salted water to the
boil for the spaghetti. Scrub the mussels
for the sauce under cold running water,
pulling off beards with a small knife.
Discard any mussels which do not close
when tapped on the counter.

Steam the mussels open: put them in
large pan, cover lightly and cook over
medium heat until done, stirring once, 4-5 minutes. Take the mussels from the pan,
reserving their liquid. Cover the mussels to keep them warm, discarding any which
are still closed.

Make the sauce: heat the olive oil in a sauté pan, add the onions and sauté until
lightly browned, 4-5 minutes. Add the garlic and continue cooking until fragrant, 1-
2 minutes. Add the reserved mussel juice to the pan, taking care to leave any
sandy deposit behind. Then add the tomatoes and bay leaf and simmer until sauce
is concentrated and just falls easily from a spoon, 5-8 minutes.

Add the spaghetti to the boiling water and simmer, stirring occasionally until al
dente, tender but still firm to the bite, 5-7 minutes. Drain, return spaghetti to the
pan and toss with olive oil. Transfer to a large serving bowl and keep warm.

Discard the bay leaf from the sauce and add the sauce to the mussels. Stir to mix
and reheat for 1 or 2 minutes. Taste and adjust the seasoning – salt may not be
necessary as the mussels are already salty. Spoon mussels and sauce over the
spaghetti, sprinkle with parsley and serve.

Prawn-stuffed ravioli in fragrant broth

I use a pasta machine to knead as well as roll out the dough, but you can, of course, do this by hand. Substitute crab or lobster for the prawns if you like.

SERVES 6

375 g/³⁄₄ pound medium raw prawns, in their shells

white of 1 egg

1 tablespoon double cream

pinch of cayenne pepper

2 spring onions

FOR THE PASTA DOUGH

300 g/10 oz flour, more if needed

3 eggs

2 teaspoons vegetable oil

1 teaspoon salt

for the fragrant broth

2 tablespoons vegetable oil

1 shallot, chopped

125 ml/4 fl oz dry white wine

2.5 litres/4 pints chicken or vegetable stock

3 star anise

7.5-cm/3-inch piece of cinnamon stick

salt and pepper

pasta machine (optional)

Peel and devein prawns, reserving shells. Make fragrant broth: heat oil in a pan. Add shallot and sauté until soft and lightly browned, 4-5 minutes. Add prawn shells and sauté, stirring, until bright pink, 2-3 minutes. Add wine, stock, star anise and cinnamon and bring to boil. Reduce heat and simmer, uncovered, for about 30 minutes.

Meanwhile, make pasta dough: sift flour on to a work surface and make a well in centre. Add eggs to well with oil and salt, and work together with fingers until well mixed. Gradually draw in flour with fingers of both hands to make crumbs. Continue working until crumbs are sticky, then press dough into a ball (work in more flour if it seems too sticky). Cover dough with an upturned bowl and let rest for 30 minutes.

Make prawn stuffing: strain broth, season to taste and bring to boil. There should be about 2 litres/3¹⁄₂ pints. Add prawns and bring just back to boil. Remove prawns with a slotted spoon and coarsely chop; set broth aside. Beat together egg white, cream, salt and pepper until mixed. Stir in chopped prawns. Finely chop white part of spring greens and stir into the stuffing. Cut greens into fine julienne strips and set aside.

Lightly flour work surface and push ball of dough away from you with heel of one hand, holding it with other. Lift from surface, give it a half-turn and push away from you again. Knead until elastic and peels from surface in one piece, 5-10 minutes. Let rest, covered with bowl, for at least 30 minutes to lose elasticity. Pat into flat round with rolling pin. Roll, turning and moving it so it doesn't stick, to postcard thickness.

Divide dough into 2-3 pieces and cover all but one with a cloth. Set pasta machine at widest setting and work dough through it. Fold into 2 or 3 and continue working through machine until satin-smooth and elastic, 8-10 minutes, dusting with flour if sticky. Pasta dough should always be firm, so don't hesitate to work in extra flour during kneading. When dough is very smooth, start reducing the machine settings until dough is a 15-cm/6-inch strip the thickness of a postcard, the thinnest setting.

Brush half dough strips lightly with water. Arrange teaspoonfuls of stuffing on half of moist dough, spaced about 5 cm/2 inches apart and leaving a 1-cm/$\frac{3}{8}$-inch border. Flip dry strip of dough over filling and press to seal between mounds of filling, pushing out any air. Using pasta wheel or chef's knife, trim edges of dough and cut between mounds to make 6-cm/2$\frac{1}{2}$-inch square ravioli. Transfer to a floured tray and lightly sprinkle with more flour. Chill for 1-2 hours, uncovered, so dough dries slightly.

Cook ravioli in a large pan of boiling salted water, a few at a time, until done, 3-4 minutes. Transfer to paper towels to drain. They can be cooked up to 30 minutes ahead. To finish, bring broth to boil. Adjust seasoning. Add 3-4 ravioli to each of 6 warmed soup bowls. Ladle over broth and scatter with reserved spring onion.

Risotto with spring greens and Parmesan

Risotto deserves the best short-grain rice – look for arborio, carnaroli or vialone nano – and Parmigiano reggiano, the aged Parmesan cheese that is only made from April to November, when the grass is lush and the cows' milk is at its richest.

SERVES 4-6 AS A MAIN COURSE

2 litres/3 $\frac{1}{2}$ pints chicken or vegetable stock, more if needed

60 g/2 oz butter

1 small onion, very finely chopped

2 shallots, very finely chopped

400 g/14 oz short-grain rice

125 ml/4 fl oz dry white wine

90 g/3 oz grated Parmesan cheese

FOR THE SPRING GREENS

750 g/1 $\frac{1}{2}$ pounds spring greens or turnip tops

3 tablespoons olive oil

1 garlic clove, lightly crushed

salt and pepper

Prepare the greens: discard any tough stems; wash and drain. Heat the oil in a large frying pan. Add the garlic and sauté just until fragrant, about 30 seconds. Discard the garlic and add the greens, salt and pepper. Cover and sweat until tender, stirring occasionally, about 5 minutes. Taste, adjust the seasoning and keep warm.

Make the risotto: bring the stock to a simmer. Meanwhile, heat all but 1 tablespoon of butter in a large, heavy-based pan. Add the onion and shallots, and cook, stirring, until soft but not brown, 3-4 minutes. Stir in the rice and sauté, stirring, until it begins to go translucent, 2-3 minutes. Stir in the wine and reduce until almost dry. Over medium heat, ladle in 250 ml/8 fl oz stock. Simmer, stirring constantly, until almost completely absorbed. Ladle in more stock, working with smaller quantities as the rice becomes tender, and continue cooking until done, 20-25 minutes.

Remove from the heat and stir in the remaining butter and half the cheese. Adjust the seasoning. Spoon some risotto into warmed bowls, top with the greens and spoon over more risotto. Sprinkle with the remaining cheese and serve.

Russian rice pilaf with lamb *Plov*

There are as many versions of *plov* as there are former Russian republics. I enjoyed this one in the home of an Uzbeki family living in Moscow. It can be made with chicken, fish, eggs or, my favourite, lamb. For flavour, the meat is cooked with the bones, which are discarded at the end. I've tried cutting down on the amount of oil, but *plov* doesn't taste the same without it, so I leave it to you.

SERVES 4-6

500 g/1 pound long-grain white rice

175 ml/6 fl oz vegetable oil

1 kg/2 pounds lamb shoulder on the bone, boned and cut into 3.75-cm/1½ -inch pieces

2 onions, coarsely chopped

2 carrots, diced

3 garlic cloves

500 g/1 pound tomatoes, peeled, seeded and chopped

2 tablespoons paprika

1 tablespoon tomato paste

salt

large heavy-based casserole

Rinse the rice and drain thoroughly. Heat the oil in the casserole until very hot. Add the lamb bones and brown thoroughly, 10-15 minutes. Reduce the heat, add the onions and cook until soft but not brown, 3-4 minutes. Add the carrots and garlic, and cook until slightly softened, 4-6 minutes. Remove the bones and vegetables.

Add the lamb pieces to the pan and brown them on all sides, 5-7 minutes. Do not crowd the pan; if necessary, browning in two batches. Return the bones and vegetables to the pan with the tomatoes and 1 litre/1⅔ pints of water. Cover and simmer for 1 hour, stirring occasionally. Discard the bones. Stir in the rice, paprika, tomato paste and a large pinch of salt.

Add more water, if necessary, to cover the rice. Bring back to the boil, cover the pan, turn the heat to medium and simmer until the water has evaporated and the rice is done, 20-25 minutes. Leave to stand for 10 minutes before stirring. Taste and adjust the seasoning with salt and paprika. Serve from the casserole. The flavour of plov mellows if it is made a day or two ahead and reheated.

Cornmeal dumplings baked with Parmesan *Gnocchi alla romana*

These simple gnocchi are made with polenta, which is left to set, then cut into shapes. Rounds are traditional, but squares are more economical. Coarse yellow cornmeal or semolina may be used for the polenta. In Italy, the polenta for gnocchi is flavoured only with Parmesan, but I've found that Dijon-style mustard really picks up the taste.

SERVES 4-6

45 g/1$\frac{1}{2}$ oz butter, melted

1 litre/1$\frac{2}{3}$ pints milk, more if
    needed

1 onion, spiked with a clove

bay leaf

1 teaspoon peppercorns

pinch of freshly grated nutmeg

salt and pepper

150 g/5 oz coarse yellow
    cornmeal or semolina

3 egg yolks

1 teaspoon Dijon-style
    mustard, more to taste

125 g/4 oz grated Parmesan
    cheese

5-cm/2-inch pastry cutter or
    glass tumbler (optional)

Thickly butter a baking sheet. In a saucepan, heat the milk with the onion, bay leaf, peppercorns, nutmeg and a little salt. Cover, bring just to the boil and leave to infuse over a low heat for 10-15 minutes. Strain and return the milk to the pan.

Gradually whisk the cornmeal or semolina into the hot milk. Bring to the boil and simmer, whisking constantly to prevent lumps, until the mixture is thick enough to pull from the sides of the pan, 8-10 minutes.

Remove the pan from the heat and beat in the egg yolks one at a time – they will cook and thicken slightly. Stir in the mustard and half the cheese, and taste for seasoning – the polenta should be highly seasoned.

Spread the polenta to form a 1-cm/$\frac{3}{8}$ -inch layer on the prepared baking sheet. Brush with the melted butter and chill until set, 1-2 hours.

When the mixture is set, preheat the oven to 230°C/450°F/gas8 and use the pastry cutter or glass to cut out 5-cm/2-inch circles, or cut 5-cm/2-inch squares. Overlap the shapes in the baking dish and sprinkle with the remaining cheese. Bake the gnocchi in the preheated oven until very hot and browned, 5-10 minutes. Serve at once.

French white bean soup with vegetables *Potage garbure*

This substantial soup from south-western France generally forms the main dish of a peasant supper, backed up by bread croûtes topped with the local Cantal cheese, which resembles sharp Cheddar. The recipe makes generous quantities, and it is even better reheated.

SERVES 6-8

75 g/2½ oz butter

2 turnips, peeled

2 large carrots, peeled

500 g/1 pound cabbage, shredded

whites of 3 leeks, thinly sliced

2-3 celery stalks, diced small

2 potatoes, peeled and cut into
   1-cm/³⁄₈ -inch dice

bunch of parsley, chopped

FOR THE BEANS

200 g/6½ oz dried white
   haricot beans or navy beans

1 onion spiked with 2 cloves

1 carrot, peeled and quartered

bouquet garni

salt and pepper

FOR THE CROÛTES

1 baguette, cut into 1-cm/
   ³⁄₈ -inch slices

2 tablespoons olive oil, bacon
   or goose fat

60 g/2 oz grated Cantal or
   Cheddar cheese

Soften the beans: soak the dried beans overnight in plenty of cold water and drain. Alternatively, put them in a saucepan with enough water to cover generously. Bring to the boil, cover the pan and remove from the heat. Leave the beans to stand for 1 hour, then drain them.

Place the softened beans, onion spiked with cloves, carrot and bouquet garni in a pan with water to cover. Cover with the lid and simmer until the beans are done, 1½–2 hours – if the beans get dry during cooking, add more water. Season with salt and pepper when the beans are almost tender. When the beans are done, discard the onion, carrot and bouquet garni.

In a large heavy pot, melt 30 g/1 oz of the butter. Add the turnips and carrots, cut into 1-cm/³⁄₈-inch dice, together with the cabbage, leeks, celery, potatoes, salt and pepper. Press a piece of buttered foil on top. Cover and sweat, stirring occasionally, until the vegetables are nearly tender but not browned, 15-20 minutes.

Add the beans and their cooking liquid, with water to cover and salt and pepper. Cover and simmer until the vegetables are very tender, 20-30 minutes. Taste the soup and adjust the seasoning.

Meanwhile, make the croûtes: preheat the oven to 200°C/400°F/gas6. Set the bread slices on an oiled baking sheet and brush the slices with oil. Bake in the preheated oven until brown, 8-10 minutes. Turn them over, sprinkle the croûtes with grated cheese and bake until well browned, 8-10 minutes.

If necessary, bring the soup back to the boil. Stir in the chopped parsley and ladle into individual bowls. Float the croûtes on top and serve at once.

Eggs

Eggs really are the cook's friend – cheap, tasty, nutritious and incredibly versatile. From childhood we love boiled eggs, preferably served with 'soldiers' of buttered toast for dipping. It's reassuring that there are so many recipes for grown-ups too – like stuffed devilled eggs, French *oeufs mayonnaise* and Scotch eggs wrapped in sausagemeat and deep-fried. In Italy, boiled eggs are served on crostini in a tarragon sauce.

Poached eggs can bolster a bowl of soup or add body to a salad such as *salade lyonnaise*. In Greece, poached eggs come in yogurt sauce; while combined with diced bacon, mushrooms and a light red wine sauce, poached eggs are transformed into *oeufs pochés en meurette*, one of the great classics of Burgundian cuisine.

A rolled omelette is a great home for a few spoonfuls of lively flavourings such as mixed herbs, ham, tomato or sautéed mushrooms. German *Königinomelett* is filled with creamed chicken and mushrooms, and Mexican *tortilla de huevo* includes tomato, avocado, onion and chilli.

A flat omelette, on the other hand, is one of my sunday night specials, a hearty dish which adapts to all sorts of fresh and cooked ingredients. Classic combinations include: Spanish *tortilla a la gallega* flavoured with pimento, potato and chorizo; Swedish *bondomelett* has onion, ham and potato; and in Italian *frittata alla romana* you'll find beans, onion and herbs.

Finally, the unbeatably comforting scrambled eggs really need very little flavouring – salt, pepper, a few chopped herbs or sautéed mushrooms are enough.

Salad with hot bacon dressing *Salade lyonnaise*

This salad of chewy winter greens wilted with hot bacon and topped with a poached egg is a favourite in the bistros of Lyons.

SERVES 4 AS A STARTER OR 2 AS
  A MAIN COURSE

**750 g/1 $\frac{1}{2}$ pounds curly endive
  (frisée) or escarole**
4 eggs
2 tablespoons vinegar

FOR THE HOT BACON DRESSING
1 tablespoon oil
**175 g/6 oz thickly sliced lean
  smoked bacon, diced**
2 garlic cloves, thinly sliced
75 ml/2 $\frac{1}{2}$ fl oz red wine vinegar
freshly ground black pepper

Discard any tough outer green leaves from the greens and pull apart the central white leaves. Wash them, dry well and put in a salad bowl.

Poach the eggs: fill a large shallow pan two-thirds full of water, add the vinegar and bring to the boil. Break the eggs one at a time into a patch of bubbling water. Regulate the heat so the water barely simmers and poach the eggs until done, 3-4 minutes. Note: it's important the yolks remain soft so that they act as a dressing for the salad leaves. With a slotted spoon, transfer the eggs to a bowl of hot water to keep them warm.

Heat the oil in a frying pan, add the bacon and fry, stirring often. When the bacon is well browned and the fat is rendered, lower the heat and add the garlic slices. Cook until the garlic is soft and fragrant but not browned, about 30 seconds. Discard some fat if you have more than 3-4 tablespoons. Pour the hot fat, bacon and garlic over the greens, and toss thoroughly so they wilt slightly.

Return the pan to the heat, add the vinegar and boil for a few seconds until reduced by half, stirring to dissolve the pan juices. Pour this over the salad and toss again. Add pepper to taste and spoon the salad on to 4 warmed individual plates or into bowls.

Drain the eggs on paper towels, set them on top of the salad and serve at once.

Eggs Florentine *Oeufs pochés à la florentine*

Classic poached *eggs à la florentine* are coated with cheese sauce, but I enjoy this version with brown butter hollandaise. Serve with sliced baguette to mop up the sauce.

SERVES 4

4 eggs
3-4 tablespoons white vinegar
1 kg/2 lb spinach
30 g/1 oz butter
1 shallot, finely chopped
salt and white pepper

FOR THE BROWN BUTTER
    HOLLANDAISE
175 g/6 oz butter
3 tablespoons water
3 egg yolks
**juice of ½ lemon, more to
    taste**

Poach the eggs and keep warm in a bowl of hot water as described opposite.

Tear the stems from the spinach leaves. Wash the leaves well in plenty of cold water and drain. Pack the spinach in a large heavy-based saucepan, cover and cook just until wilted, stirring occasionally, 3-4 minutes. Let the spinach cool, then squeeze it in your fists to extract as much liquid as possible.

Melt the butter in a large frying pan over medium heat. Add the shallot and cook until soft, 1-2 minutes. Add the drained spinach and sauté, stirring until hot and all liquid has evaporated, 1-2 minutes. Taste, adjust the seasoning and keep warm.

To make the brown butter hollandaise, first brown the butter. In a small heavy pan, heat the butter gently, skimming the froth from its surface. Continue simmering, stirring occasionally, until the butter stops sputtering and the sediment in the pan is golden with a nutty aroma, 5-7 minutes. Pour into a bowl and let cool to tepid.

Wipe the pan with paper towel, add the water and egg yolks with a little seasoning, and whisk until thoroughly combined and the eggs lighten slightly in colour. Set over a low heat or in a water bath and whisk vigorously to form a mousse creamy and thick enough to hold a ribbon trail for 3 seconds, 3-5 minutes. The pan base should never be more than hand-hot or the yolks will cook too quickly.

Take the pan from the heat. Whisk in the brown butter, a little at a time, until the sauce starts to thicken slightly. Continue whisking in the butter in a slow steady stream, leaving the brown sediment at the bottom of the bowl. Stir in the lemon juice and adjust the seasoning.

Spoon a layer of spinach on 4 warmed individual plates. Drain the eggs and pat them dry on paper towels. Set the eggs on the beds of spinach. Spoon the brown butter hollandaise sauce over the eggs and serve at once.

Fried eggs with tomato-chilli sauce *Huevos rancheros*

The seeds and internal pale membrane hold much of a chilli's heat. To control the spice of this tomato-chilli sauce, I generally discard both seeds and membrane, but if you have macho taste buds, you can include them.

SERVES 4

**4 corn or flour tortillas,
   15 cm/6 inches across
75 ml/2 ½ fl oz vegetable oil
4 eggs
30 g/1 oz grated sharp Cheddar
   or Monterey Jack cheese
1 tablespoon chopped
   coriander**

FOR THE TOMATO-CHILLI SAUCE

**½ small onion, cut into pieces
3-4 small fresh hot green chilli
   peppers, seeded and cut into
   pieces
2 garlic cloves, cut into pieces
750 g/1 ½ pounds tomatoes,
   peeled, seeded and cut into
   pieces
1 tablespoon vegetable oil
salt**

Make the tomato-chilli sauce: put the onion, chillies and garlic in a food processor and work until quite finely chopped. Add the tomatoes and work to a coarse purée. Heat the oil in a medium frying pan. Add the tomato purée to the pan and simmer, stirring constantly until the sauce thickens enough to coat the back of a spoon, 8-10 minutes. Remove from the heat, taste and adjust seasoning with salt. Keep warm.

Meanwhile, heat a large heavy-based frying pan over high heat until very hot. Roast the tortillas in the dry pan one at a time until hot and starting to brown, 2-3 seconds on each side. Set them on 4 warmed plates.

Reduce the heat under the pan to medium. Add the oil and heat until a drop of water sizzles. Break an egg into a cup and slide it into the pan. Repeat with the remaining eggs and fry over medium heat, basting constantly until done, 2-3 minutes. Using a slotted spoon, set the eggs on the tortillas.

Reheat the sauce if necessary and spoon it over the eggs to cover the whites and tortillas. Sprinkle with cheese and coriander and serve at once.

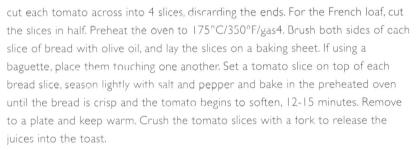

Scrambled eggs with fresh herbs on tomato toasts

No matter what kind of herbs you have available – chives, tarragon, chervil, even parsley – as long as they're fresh, they'll make all the difference in this simple dish.

SERVES 4

8 eggs

2 tablespoons chopped mixed herbs as above, plus sprigs for garnish

30 g/1 oz butter

FOR THE TOMATO TOASTS

2 large tomatoes

8 slices of French baguette or 4 slices of a larger French loaf, cut 1 cm/³⁄₈ inch thick

2 tablespoons olive oil

salt and pepper

Make the tomato toasts:
cut each tomato across into 4 slices, discarding the ends. For the French loaf, cut the slices in half. Preheat the oven to 175°C/350°F/gas4. Brush both sides of each slice of bread with olive oil, and lay the slices on a baking sheet. If using a baguette, place them touching one another. Set a tomato slice on top of each bread slice, season lightly with salt and pepper and bake in the preheated oven until the bread is crisp and the tomato begins to soften, 12-15 minutes. Remove to a plate and keep warm. Crush the tomato slices with a fork to release the juices into the toast.

Whisk the eggs with salt and pepper until slightly frothy. Stir in the chopped herbs. Melt the butter in a heavy saucepan (copper if possible). Add the eggs and stir constantly with a wooden spoon over very low heat until cooked to your taste, at least 8-10 minutes. The more slowly the eggs cook, the better they'll be. Note: they do continue to cook in the pan after it's been removed from the heat.

Taste the eggs and adjust the seasoning. Spoon them over the tomato toasts, garnish with herb sprigs and serve at once.

Blue cheese and walnut omelette

Any moist blue cheese works well in this omelette – strong or mild.

SERVES 2-3

5-6 eggs
45 g/1 $\frac{1}{2}$ oz butter
1 small onion, chopped
salt and pepper
125 g/4 oz blue cheese,
  crumbled
30 g/1 oz walnuts, chopped
1 tablespoon double cream

23-cm/9-inch omelette pan

Melt one-third of the butter in a frying pan. Add the onion, salt and pepper, and sauté over moderate heat until soft but not brown, 3-4 minutes. Take the pan from the heat and stir in the cheese, walnuts and cream.

Whisk the eggs in a bowl with a little salt and pepper until slightly foamy. In the omelette pan, heat the remaining butter over fairly high heat until it stops sputtering and just starts to brown. Add the eggs and stir briskly with a fork, pulling the cooked egg from the sides to the centre, until they start to thicken, 20-25 seconds. Stir in the blue cheese mix and continue cooking, stirring constantly, until the egg is lightly set. Stop stirring and leave the omelette to brown on the underside and cook until soft or firm, according to taste, 1-1 $\frac{1}{2}$ minutes.

Tip the pan towards you and fold over one side of omelette. Roll and slide the omelette towards you on to a warmed platter. Serve at once.

Fish soufflé with curry sauce

This soufflé is cooked for longer than usual, so it is fairly firm in the centre. You'll need a full-flavoured fish, such as cod, snapper or salmon.

SERVES 4

300 g/10 oz cooked flaked fish
60 ml/2 fl oz double cream
pinch of dry mustard
4 egg yolks
6 egg whites

Preheat the oven to 190°C/375°F/gas5 and butter the soufflé dish.

Make the béchamel sauce: scald the milk with the onion, bay leaf and peppercorns. Cover and leave to infuse off the heat, 10-15 minutes. In a heavy-based saucepan, melt the butter, whisk in the flour and cook, stirring, until the

FOR THE BÉCHAMEL SAUCE
500 ml/16 fl oz milk
1 large slice of onion
1 bay leaf
1/2 teaspoon black peppercorns
45 g/1 ½ oz butter
30 g/1 oz flour
salt and white pepper
generous pinch of nutmeg

FOR THE CURRY SAUCE
30 g/1 oz butter
2 shallots, finely chopped
2-3 teaspoons curry powder
60 ml/2 fl oz double cream
125 ml/4 fl oz milk

1.25-litre/2-pint soufflé dish

flour is foaming but not browned, about 1 minute. Off the heat, strain in the hot milk, whisk well, then bring to the boil, whisking constantly until the sauce thickens. Season to taste with salt, pepper and nutmeg and leave to simmer 1-2 minutes.

Pour half the béchamel sauce into a bowl and reserve. Beat the fish, cream and mustard into the remaining sauce, taste and adjust the seasoning – the mixture should be highly seasoned. Heat the fish mixture until very hot, then take from the heat and beat in the egg yolks so they cook and thicken the mixture slightly.

In a bowl (copper if possible), beat the egg whites until stiff. Reheat the fish mixture until it is hot to the touch, add about one-quarter of the egg whites and stir until well mixed. Add this to remaining egg whites and fold together as gently as possible. Pour the mixture into prepared soufflé dish and smooth the top. Bake in the preheated oven until the soufflé is puffed and brown, 25-30 minutes.

Meanwhile, make the curry sauce: melt the butter in a saucepan, add the shallots and curry powder and cook gently, stirring occasionally, 3-4 minutes. Whisk in the reserved béchamel sauce, cream and milk, and bring to the boil. Taste and adjust the seasoning. Serve the soufflé as soon as it is ready, passing the curry sauce separately.

Twice-baked cheese and herb soufflés

This recipe is an exception to the rule that soufflés must be served at once. The mixture is baked, left to cool, then unmoulded and coated with a cream sauce.

SERVES 6

60 g/2 oz butter

30 g/1 oz flour

375 ml/12 fl oz milk

pinch of nutmeg

salt and pepper

375 ml/12 fl oz single cream

5 egg yolks

100 g/3 $\frac{1}{4}$ oz grated cheese (a mixture of Parmesan and Gruyère is best, but you can just use a sharp Cheddar)

bunch of chives, chopped

whites of 6 eggs

six 250-ml/8-fl oz ramekins and six 15-cm/6-inch gratin dishes

Generously butter the ramekins and chill. In a heavy pan, melt the butter, whisk in the flour and cook until foaming but not browned, about 1 minute. Whisk in the milk, nutmeg, salt and pepper, and bring to the boil, stirring constantly, until thick. Simmer for 2 minutes. Take from the heat and transfer about one-third to a small pan. Pour over the cream and set aside. Whisk the egg yolks one at a time into the remaining sauce so they cook in its heat and thicken it slightly. Take from the heat and whisk in the cheese and chives, reserving 3-4 tablespoons of cheese and 1 tablespoon of chives. Adjust the seasoning – it should be highly seasoned. Cover with cling film or rub the surface with butter to prevent a skin forming.

Preheat the oven to 175°C/350°F/gas4. Bring a roasting pan of water to the boil on the stove. Beat the egg whites until stiff. Warm the sauce gently until the pan is hot to the touch. (Don't overheat or the cheese will become stringy.) Add about a quarter of the egg whites and stir until well mixed. Fold into the remaining egg whites as gently as possible. Use to fill the ramekins and smooth tops with a palette knife. Run a thumb around the edge of each dish so the soufflé will rise straight. Set the ramekins in the pan of water. Bring back to the boil on the hob and transfer to the oven. Bake until the soufflés are puffed, browned and just set in the centre, 15-20 minutes. They should rise well above the dish rims. Remove from the water bath and let cool – they'll shrink back into the ramekins, pulling away slightly from the sides.

Turn each soufflé out into a gratin dish. Whisk the cream with the reserved sauce until smooth and bring just to the boil. Season and pour on top of the soufflés, allowing it to pool around sides. Sprinkle with the reserved cheese. They can be prepared to this point up to 24 hours ahead and kept covered in the refrigerator.

Preheat the oven to 220°C/425°F/gas7. Bake the soufflés until browned, slightly puffed and sauce bubbling, 5-7 minutes. Sprinkle with the reserved chives to serve.

Desserts

Desserts bring out the ingenuity in every cook and every cuisine. After all, most sweet dishes are based on very much the same ingredients – eggs, sugar, milk, cream and fruit – but just think what can be done with them. Cream alone can be whipped and variously flavoured to give us delights like lemon and sherry syllabub or made into fools mixed with puréed fruit. Adding in eggs opens up the wonders of meringue, soufflés and batter puddings, each of which are capable of endlessly inventive variations – like the classic French *gâteau progrès*, in which meringue is softened by the addition of ground nuts or *oeufs à la neige* where spoonfuls of soft meringue are poached and served floating on custard – another miracle from the egg.

Various fruits can be poached, sautéed, stewed, grilled, fried, puréed or baked in tarts and pies to make memorable last courses, from homely blackberry and apple pie, to festive cherries jubilee flamed in brandy, or even traditional pears belle helène, with ice cream and chocolate sauce.

Mention of ice cream and chocolate sauce opens up two vast new theatres of creation: from ices flavoured with crystallized ginger, cardamom, Christmas pudding, green tea or muscat wine, to sundaes piled with fruit and bombes stuffed with candied fruit and nuts.

Chocolate can be married with almost every flavour known and, as well as making that most useful of sauces, can come in the form of mousses, terrines, crunchy coatings, cakes and, of course, the incomparable truffle.

Cherries jubilee

Flambéed cherries are most famous served over ice cream as a 'jubilee' celebration, but if you reduce the sugar they are also delicious with duck or pork. Dark sweet cherries such as Bing are best for flambéing.

SERVES 6

750 g/1 1/2 pounds dark
   sweet cherries
1 litre/1 2/3 pints vanilla
   ice cream, for serving
30 g/1 oz butter
45 g/1 1/2 oz sugar
1 tablespoon redcurrant
   jelly
175 ml/6 fl oz brandy

Marinated cherries

If you'd rather not have the theatrics of flambéing, simply marinate the cherries in the brandy sweetened with the sugar overnight, stirring from time to time. You can serve these cold or warm them gently in a saucepan. For an even stronger flavour, spoon 2 tablespoons of kirsch over the cherries just before serving.

Scoop the vanilla ice cream into 6 chilled coupe glasses or attractive serving bowls and store them in the freezer. Stone the cherries.

Melt the butter in a sauté pan, stir in the sugar, and heat gently until the sugar dissolves completely, stirring occasionally, about 1 minute. Add the cherries and sauté over high heat for 1 minute. Add the redcurrant jelly and stir until dissolved. Simmer until the cherries are almost tender, 3-5 minutes.

To flame the cherries: warm the brandy in a small saucepan, then set it alight. Pour it, flaming, over the cherries and baste them.

When the flames have died down completely, spoon the hot cherries and their delicious sauce over the ice cream and serve at once.

Cherries jubilee

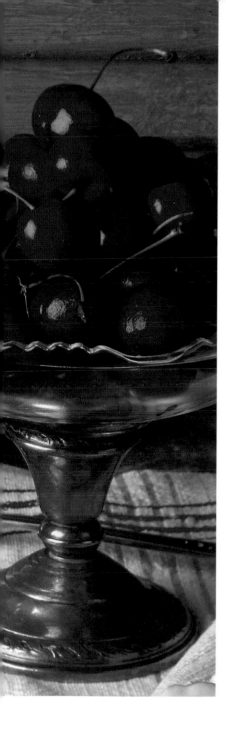

Danish berry soup *Rødgrød*

The dessert soup called rødgrød is popular throughout Scandinavia. I like to make it with a combination of firm berries that need to be simmered, such as redcurrants or blueberries, and softer fruits like strawberries and raspberries, which should be scarcely cooked at all.

SERVES 4-6

175 g/6 oz strawberries, hulled
250 g/½ pound raspberries
250 g/½ pound redcurrants or blueberries
50 g/1¾ oz sugar, more to taste
500 ml/16 fl oz water
2 tablespoons arrowroot mixed to a paste with 60 ml/2 fl oz water
juice of 1 lemon (optional)
double cream and caster sugar for serving

Cut the strawberries in pieces about the same size as the raspberries.

Combine the sugar and water in a pan and heat gently, stirring occasionally, until the sugar dissolves. Bring to the boil and simmer for 2 minutes. Add the redcurrants or blueberries and simmer until very soft, 8-12 minutes.

Let cool slightly, then purée in a food processor or with an immersion blender. Return to the pan and bring just to the boil. Whisk in the arrowroot paste – the purée will thicken at once. Stir in the berry fruit and simmer, stirring gently, until soft, 3-5 minutes.

Take from the heat and add lemon juice or more sugar if needed. Let cool, then pour into a 4 individual bowls and chill thoroughly. It thickens considerably on standing but should remain pourable. Thin with a little cold water if necessary. Serve chilled, with cream and sugar.

Rhubarb compote

Other fruit leaves and herbs to use in this compote include elderflowers, rose, geranium, comfrey or lemon balm. If fresh leaves are not available, you can use herbal tea bags. Almond biscuits make a pleasant accompaniment to the compote.

SERVES 4-6

1 kg/2 pounds rhubarb stalks

250 ml/8 fl oz water

250 ml/8 fl oz white wine

400 g/14 oz sugar

2 tablespoons fresh blackberry leaves

2 tablespoons fresh strawberry leaves

2 tablespoons fresh raspberry leaves

1 Ceylon tea bag

500 g/1 pound strawberries

Peel the outer skin from the rhubarb stalks. Slice the stalks thinly and put them in a stainless steel bowl. Combine the wine and sugar in a saucepan with 250ml/8 fl oz water. Heat the mixture, stirring occasionally, until the sugar has completely dissolved, then bring to the boil. Add the blackberry, strawberry and raspberry leaves, together with the tea bag. Remove from the heat, cover, and let infuse for 15 minutes.

Strain through a fine sieve and bring back to the boil. Add the rhubarb and bring back to the boil again. Pour into a bowl, cover with cling film and then with foil. Note: the rhubarb continues to cook in the insulated bowl. Let stand until cool. Chill the fruit for at least 6 hours – the flavour improves on standing.

Hull and halve the strawberries, rinsing them only if they are sandy. Just before serving, add the strawberries to the compote and taste, adding more sugar if necessary. Spoon into coupe glasses and serve chilled.

Baked banana pudding

This dessert can stand alone, but is even better with **Coconut ice cream** (page 134).

SERVES 6

8 bananas
   (about 1.4 kg/3 pounds)
1 tablespoon sesame seeds
1 teaspoon lemon juice
2 tablespoons rum
1 tablespoon sugar

6 individual 15-cm/6-in gratin
   dishes

FOR THE PASTRY CREAM
175 ml/6 fl oz milk
1 vanilla pod, split
2 eggs, separated
2 tablespoons sugar
1 tablespoon flour

Preheat the oven to 220°C/425°F/gas7. Brush the gratin dishes with butter. In a small frying pan, toast the sesame seeds on a low heat, stirring them until browned, 2-3 minutes. Peel 6 of the bananas and split them lengthwise. Set the banana halves cut side down around the edge of the dishes.

Make the pastry cream: scald the milk in a medium saucepan with the vanilla pod, cover and leave to infuse off the heat, 5-10 minutes. Meanwhile, beat the egg yolks (reserving the whites) with the sugar until thick and light. Stir in the flour. Whisk the milk into the egg mixture and return it to the saucepan. Cook over a low heat, whisking constantly, until the cream comes to the boil and thickens. Simmer, stirring, for 1-2 minutes. Remove the vanilla pod and set the pastry cream aside. The vanilla pod can be rinsed and used again.

Make the pudding: peel the remaining 2 bananas and purée them in a food processor with the lemon juice, rum and vanilla. Stir the purée into the pastry cream.

Stiffly beat the reserved egg whites, preferably in a copper bowl. Add the sugar and continue beating until the whites are glossy and hold a long peak, 30-60 seconds.

If necessary, heat the banana mixture until hot to the touch. Stir in about a quarter of the egg whites. Add this mixture to the remaining egg whites and fold them together as lightly as possible. Spoon the mixture into the prepared gratin dishes, piling it inside the bananas.

Bake in the preheated oven until the pudding is puffed and the bananas are done, 12-15 minutes. Sprinkle with the toasted sesame seeds and serve at once.

Red wine and berry terrine

When sliced, this colourful and tasty fruit terrine reveals a vivid mosaic of fruit held together with a red wine jelly. A fruity red wine such as a Zinfandel or a Beaujolais is best. For a winter version, substitute sliced poached pears, figs, grapes and segmented oranges for the berries. Serve the jelly with a bowl of whipped Chantilly cream.

SERVES 6-8

250 g/½ pound strawberries

125 g/4 oz blueberries

125 g/4 oz raspberries

125 g/4 oz blackberries

1.5-litre/2⅓-pint terrine mould

FOR THE WINE JELLY

15 g/½ oz powdered gelatine

250 ml/8 fl oz water

100 g/3¼ oz sugar, or more to taste

1 bottle (750 ml/1¼ pints) fruity red wine

Make the wine jelly: sprinkle the gelatine over half the water in a medium bowl and leave until softened and spongy, about 5 minutes. In a small pan, heat the sugar and the remaining water, stirring occasionally, until the sugar is dissolved. Bring the syrup just to the boil, pour over the gelatine and stir until melted. Stir in the wine.

Assemble the terrine: put the terrine mould in a roasting pan half-filled with ice and water. Pour a 1-cm/⅜-inch layer of the gelatine mixture into the mould and leave it to set.

Meanwhile, hull the strawberries and halve them if large. Pick over the blueberries, raspberries and blackberries. Rinse the berries only if they are sandy, drying them well. Mix the berries in a bowl.

When the layer of jelly is set, spread the berries on top. Add the remaining gelatine mixture, shaking and tapping the mould so the mixture fills all the spaces between the fruit. Note: be sure the fruit is completely covered with jelly, so the terrine sits flat when unmoulded. Cover and chill until set, at least 6 hours.

Unmould the terrine: dip the mould in a bowl of warm water 5-10 seconds. Using the point of a knife or your fingers, gently ease the terrine away from the edges of the mould. Set a baking sheet or small chopping board on top, turn over and lift off the terrine mould. With a serrated knife, cut the terrine into 1.25-cm/½ -inch slices and transfer to individual plates. The colourful berries, highlighted by the red jelly, are their own decoration.

Hazelnut and pear soufflé

Toasted hazelnuts add flavour and stabilize the fruit juice, so the soufflé holds well.

SERVES 4

75 g/2$\frac{1}{2}$ oz hazelnuts

1 ripe pear

$\frac{1}{2}$ lemon

whites of 4 eggs

**1$\frac{1}{2}$ tablespoons caster
    sugar**

**icing sugar (for
    sprinkling)**

FOR THE THICK PASTRY
    CREAM

150 ml/5 fl oz milk

1 vanilla pod, split

2 egg yolks

**1$\frac{1}{2}$ tablespoons caster
    sugar**

2 tablespoons flour

**1.25-litre/2-pint soufflé
    dish**

Preheat the oven to 175°C/350°F/gas4. Brush the dish well with melted butter. Spread the nuts on a baking sheet and toast in the oven until lightly brown, 12-15 minutes, stirring once. Let cool slightly, then rub in a cloth to remove skins. Grind in a processor (do not overwork or they will be oily). Increase oven to 220°C/425°F/gas7.

Make the pastry cream: scald the milk with the vanilla, cover and infuse off the heat for 5-10 minutes. Meanwhile, beat the egg yolks and sugar until thick and light. Stir in the flour. Whisk in the milk and return to the pan. Cook over low heat, whisking constantly, until it boils and thickens. Simmer, stirring, for 1-2 minutes. Strain into a bowl. Let cool slightly and stir in nuts.

Peel, quarter and core the pear. Rub with the cut surface of the lemon and purée until smooth. Stir into the nut mixture.

Stiffly beat the egg whites. Add the sugar and continue beating until glossy and holding a long peak, 30-60 seconds.

If necessary, heat the nut mixture until hot to the touch. Stir in about a quarter of the egg whites. Add this to the remaining egg whites and fold together as lightly as possible. Spoon into the dish and smooth the top. Run a thumb around the edge so it rises in a hat shape.

Bake until puffed and brown, 15-18 minutes. It should be slightly soft in the centre. Sprinkle with icing sugar, set on a plate lined with a napkin, and serve.

Mango and lime fool

The English dessert of 'fool', based on whipped cream, is ancient, dating back to the Renaissance. This tropical version is delicate and airy – perfect for a warm summer evening. Be sure to use very ripe mangoes.

SERVES 4-6

- **1 kg/2 pounds mangoes**
- **3 limes**
- **1 tablespoon sugar, or more to taste**
- **250 ml/8 fl oz double cream**

Prepare the mangoes: cut a vertical slice about 6mm/¼ inch from either side of each mango stem, clearing the flat stone inside. Set each of these thick slices skin side down and score the flesh in a lattice pattern, cutting through the flesh but not the skin. Holding the mango flesh upward, push the centre of the skin with your thumbs to turn it inside out, opening the cut flesh to reveal cubes. Cut the cubes from the skin. Trim the remaining flesh from the stone with a knife, discarding the skin.

Grate the zest from the limes. Halve the limes, cut 4-6 thin slices from one half, and reserve these for decoration. Squeeze the juice from the remaining lime halves. Purée the mango flesh with the lime zest and juice in a food processor, or work the mango through a sieve and stir in the zest and juice. Stir in sugar to taste.

Whip the cream until it holds a soft peak. Stir a little into the mango purée to lighten it. Add the purée to the remaining cream and fold together. Taste again, adjusting the amount of sugar and lime juice. Pile the mixture in stemmed glasses and chill for at least 2 hours or overnight – the flavour mellows on standing.

Just before serving, top each fool with a lime slice.

Hazelnut and pear soufflé

Poached pears in sweet wine with ginger

Many variations can be played on this basic recipe. I'm fond of using a cinnamon stick or crushed peppercorns instead of ginger, and substituting red for white wine to give a pink blush to the pears. For poaching, it is important to use firm pears which hold up.

SERVES 4

4 pears (about 750 g/1½ pounds)

1 lemon

1 bottle (750 ml/1¾ pints) Sauternes or other good sweet white wine

2.5-cm/1-inch piece of fresh ginger, thinly sliced

50 g/1¾ oz sugar

Pare the zest from the lemon and squeeze the juice from one half. Peel the pears, leaving stems intact, and rub with the remaining lemon half to prevent discoloration. Using a vegetable peeler or pointed teaspoon, scoop out the fibrous cores without breaking open the pears. Cut a thin slice from base of each pear so they will sit upright.

Combine the wine, lemon zest and juice, ginger and sugar in a small deep pan with 250ml/8 fl oz water. Heat, stirring occasionally, until the sugar dissolves, then bring to the boil. Add the pears and press a piece of greaseproof paper on top to keep them submerged. Bring just to the boil, reduce heat and poach until done, 25-35 minutes.

Lift the pears from the pan, using the stems as handles, and stand them upright in a serving bowl or individual bowls. Discard the lemon zest and ginger, and boil the liquid until syrupy and reduced by about half, 10-15 minutes. Spoon this syrup over the pears. Cover and leave to cool. Serve at room temperature or chilled.

Apricot snow

This recipe can be adapted for many different fruits. Apricots colour the snow pale orange, while red plums make it rosy. Serve the snow with crisp biscuits.

SERVES 6

750 g/1 ½ pounds apricots, halved and stoned

200 g/6 ½ oz sugar, more if needed

pared zest and juice of 1 orange

white of 1 egg

6 mint sprigs

six 250-ml/8-fl oz parfait glasses

In a sauté pan or shallow saucepan, add the sugar to 250ml/8 fl oz water, reserving 3-4 tablespoons of sugar. Heat, stirring, until the sugar dissolves. Bring just to the boil, take from heat and add the apricot halves and orange zest. Cut a round of waxed paper the size of pan and press this on the fruit. Return to the heat and poach the fruit over low heat until just tender, 5-7 minutes. Using a slotted spoon, remove the apricot halves and reserve.

Continue cooking the remaining apricots until soft enough to purée, 3-5 minutes longer. Let cool to tepid, discard the orange zest and purée the fruit with the syrup in a food processor or blender. You should have about 375 ml/12 fl oz. Chill the purée.

Beat the egg white just until foamy, 1-2 minutes. Beat in the reserved sugar, a tablespoonful at a time, then continue beating until the egg white is glossy and forms a long peak when whisk is lifted, about 1 minute more. Beat in the chilled apricot purée and orange juice. Continue beating until the snow is smooth, light and slightly thickened, 3-5 minutes. Taste and add more sugar if needed.

Spoon the snow and reserved whole apricots into parfait glasses in 2-3 alternating layers. Top each glass with a slice of poached apricot and a mint sprig. Chill for at least 1 hour before serving.

Fig toasts

Fresh figs, with their deep red flesh and delicate flavour, call for the simplest treatment. Here, they are sautéed briefly in butter and sugar, then topped with browned almonds to make a perfect summer dessert. For a luscious treat, substitute mascarpone for the yogurt.

SERVES 4

12 medium figs
 (750 kg/1 ½ pounds)
4 slices of brioche
 or challah (page 145),
 cut 2.5-cm/1-in thick
100 g/3 ¼ oz sugar
45 g/1 ½ oz butter
125 g/4 oz plain yogurt, stirred
 until smooth
45 g/1 ½ oz slivered almonds

Preheat the oven to 260°C/500°F/gas 10 or its highest possible setting. Toast the bread: lay the bread slices directly on the oven rack and toast in the preheated oven until golden, 4-5 minutes. Place the slices of toast on 4 warmed plates.

Meanwhile trim the stems off the figs. Slice the figs in half and dip the halves in sugar, turning them so they are well coated. Set aside.

In a frying pan, heat 1 tablespoon of the butter, add the almonds and sauté until golden brown, 2-3 minutes. Set them aside.

Heat the remaining butter in the pan until foaming. Add the figs, cut side down, and sauté until done, turning once, 3-5 minutes.

Set the figs on the toast and spoon over the pan juices. Top each toast with yogurt and a sprinkling of toasted almonds. Serve at once so the toast stays crisp.

Champagne fruit fritters

This recipe features two fruits which fall neatly into rings – apple and pineapple. There's no need to use real champagne as any sparkling white wine will do. You'll get the same lightness with soda water – though not, of course, the same taste!

MAKES ABOUT 18 FRITTERS

1 pineapple, about
  750 g/1 ½ pounds
2 tart apples, about
  500 g/1 pound
2 tablespoons sugar
1 tablespoon ground cinnamon
vegetable oil, for deep-frying
icing sugar, for sprinkling

FOR THE CHAMPAGNE FRITTER
  BATTER
250 g/8 oz flour
½ teaspoon salt
375 ml/12 fl oz champagne,
  more if needed

Make the champagne fritter batter: sift the flour and salt into a bowl and make a well in the centre. Pour the champagne into the well and stir gently with a whisk, gradually drawing in the flour, to make a smooth batter. It should fall easily from the spoon, so add more champagne if necessary. Do not whisk vigorously or the batter will be heavy. Cover and let stand at room temperature for 30-60 minutes.

Peel and core the pineapple: slice off the plume and stem ends. Cut away the peel in strips, following the curve of the fruit and cutting deep enough to remove the eyes with the pineapple peel. Slice the pineapple into 1.25-cm/½-inch thick rounds. Core the rounds with a small pastry cutter or knife to make rings.

Peel the apples and scoop out their flower and stem ends. Remove the seeds and central core with an apple corer or small knife. Slice each apple into 1-cm/⅜-inch thick rings, discarding the thin end slices.

Combine the sugar and cinnamon in a small bowl. Lay the apple slices on a tray, sprinkle with the sugar and cinnamon mixture, turn the slices and sprinkle the other sides. Repeat with the pineapple rings.

In a wok or deep-fryer, heat the oil to 190°C/375°F. One by one, dip the apple slices in batter so they are completely coated. Lift out and let excess batter drain for 1-2 seconds. Lower the pieces into the hot oil and deep-fry until done, turning once and stirring gently with a draining spoon so the fruit cooks evenly, 3-4 minutes. Fry the rings in 3-4 batches so the pan is not crowded. Drain on paper towels and keep warm, uncovered, in a low oven with the door open. Fry the remaining apple rings in the same way, followed by the pineapple rings.

Sprinkle the warm fritters with icing sugar and serve at once.

Cherry batter pudding *Clafoutis limousin*

For flavour, this pudding from central France is generally made without stoning the local tart black cherries. If you choose to leave the stones in, do warn your guests.

SERVES 6

500 g/1 pound tart cherries
30 g/1 oz flour
60 g/2 oz granulated sugar
pinch of salt
4 eggs
250 ml/8 fl oz milk
60 ml/2 fl oz Cognac or 3
**   tablespoons kirsch**
icing sugar for sprinkling

1.5-litre/2½-pint shallow
**   baking dish**

Preheat the oven to 175°C/350°F/gas4. Butter the baking dish and sprinkle it with granulated sugar. Stone the cherries if you prefer. Spread the cherries in the dish.

Make the batter: sift the flour, sugar and salt into a bowl and make a well in the centre. Add the eggs to the well and stir with a whisk until mixed. Stir in half the milk, then continue stirring to draw in the flour and make a smooth mixture. Stir in the remaining milk to make a smooth batter.

Pour the batter over the cherries and bake in the preheated oven until the clafoutis is done, 35-45 minutes. Sprinkle the Cognac or kirsch over the hot pudding and serve hot or warm. The clafoutis will sink slightly as it cools. Sprinkle with icing sugar just before serving.

Orange, lemon and lime custards

Classic *pots de crème* come in threes, flavoured variously with vanilla, coffee and chocolate. Here I'm suggesting a Californian touch of citrus. Two pots form a modest serving; with three, everyone tastes each flavour.

SERVES 4-6

3 oranges

4 lemons

4 limes

1 litre/1$\frac{2}{3}$ pints milk

12 egg yolks

150 g/5 oz sugar

FOR THE CANDIED ZEST

150 g/5 oz sugar

175 ml/6 fl oz water

12 individual mousse pots with lids, or small ramekins

Preheat the oven to 175°C/350°F/gas4. For a water bath: line a roasting pan with a folded dish towel, add about 4 cm/1½ inches water and bring to the boil on the hob. Pare 2-3 wide pieces of zest from each type of fruit and slice into julienne strips. Grate the remaining zest into three separate bowls. Scald the milk.

Meanwhile, beat the egg yolks and sugar until thickened and light, 3-5 minutes. Whisk the hot milk into the egg mixture, then divide the mixture evenly into the three bowls of grated citrus zest. Leave to infuse for 10-15 minutes.

Strain the custards into individual pots or ramekins – there should be four pots of each flavour. Set the pots in the water bath and cover with lids or a sheet of cardboard. Bring the water bath back to the boil on the hob and transfer to the preheated oven. Bake until the custard is done, 15-20 minutes. Remove the pots from the water bath and let them cool.

Meanwhile, candy the citrus julienne: blanch the julienne strips one fruit at a time in a small pot of boiling water for 2 minutes, then drain. In a separate pan, gently heat the sugar and water until the sugar dissolves to make a syrup. Pour off and reserve two-thirds of the syrup. Add one batch of blanched zest to the remaining syrup in the pan and simmer until all the water has evaporated and the zest is translucent, 8-10 minutes. Lift the zest out with a fork, spread on greaseproof paper and leave to cool. Repeat with the remaining syrup and zests.

Just before serving, top each pot or ramekin with a few strips of candied zest to identify the flavour. Serve the custards chilled.

Panettone bread pudding

This version of bread and butter pudding, which I first came across at an Italian restaurant in London, is one of our very favourite desserts. When I make it myself, I often add some grappa, a pungent Italian eau-de-vie.

SERVES 6-8

500 g/1 pound panettone

3-4 tablespoons butter

500 ml/16 fl oz double cream

125 ml/4 fl oz milk

75 ml/2$\frac{1}{2}$ fl oz grappa or Cognac

4 eggs, lightly beaten

2 tablespoons sugar

pinch of salt

2-litre/3$\frac{1}{4}$ pint soufflé dish

Preheat the oven to 160°C/325°F/gas3. Generously butter the soufflé dish. Cut the panettone into quarters lengthwise, then cut each quarter across in 2.5-cm/1-inch fan-shaped slices. Spread one side of each slice with butter. Line the bottom and sides of the soufflé dish with the panettone, buttered side inwards. Arrange the remaining slices in layers in the centre of the dish.

In a medium bowl, whisk the cream, milk, grappa, eggs, sugar and salt until foamy. Pour this mixture over the panettone. Press the slices down so they are completely submerged and let stand for 10 minutes so the bread soaks up the liquid.

Cover the dish loosely with foil and bake in the preheated oven for 30 minutes. Uncover and continue baking until done, 30-40 minutes more. Serve the pudding warm.

Panettone bread pudding

Indian creamed rice *Kheer*

Not to be confused with rustic rice puddings, *kheer* is a dessert deemed worthy of royal banquets and newlywed brides. *Vark* – silver or gold leaf – is available at Indian speciality shops and adds the appropriate touch of ceremony.

SERVES 6

1.5 litres/2⅓ pints milk, or
   more if needed
75 g/2½ oz short-grain rice
4 cardamom pods, crushed
2.5-cm/1-inch piece of
   cinnamon stick
2 whole cloves
75 g/2½ oz sugar
45 g/1½ oz sultanas
2 tablespoons rose water
60 g/2 oz sliced almonds,
   toasted
45 g/1½ oz blanched
   pistachios, chopped
silver leaf (optional)

muslin

In a large saucepan, bring the milk to the boil. Stir the rice into the milk. Cook, uncovered, over low heat, stirring often, 15 minutes.

Tie the cardamom, cinnamon and cloves in a piece of muslin and add to the rice. Continue simmering, uncovered, stirring occasionally for 1 hour. Add the sugar and raisins, and continue cooking until the raisins are plump and the rice is done, 45-60 minutes.

Remove the rice from the heat and discard the spice bag. Stir in the rose water together with three-quarters of the almonds and taste, adding more sugar if you like. Transfer to a bowl, cover and chill, at least 12 hours or overnight. The flavour will improve and the pudding will thicken on standing.

To serve: if the pudding is thick, stir in a little milk. Spoon into individual dishes and sprinkle with the reserved almonds, pistachios and *vark*, if using.

Greek fritters with honey syrup *Loukoumades*

These fritters are traditionally served on November 30th, the day of St Andrew, patron saint of Greece. *Loukoumades* **may simply be dipped in honey syrup, or left to soak for a softer, richer effect.**

MAKES ABOUT 36 FRITTERS

2 teaspoons/7 g/¼ oz active
  dry yeast
125 ml/4 fl oz warm water, or
  more if needed
375 g/¾ pound flour
½ teaspoon salt
125 ml/4 fl oz milk
3 eggs
vegetable oil for deep-frying
ground cinnamon for sprinkling
freshly grated nutmeg for
  sprinkling

FOR THE HONEY SYRUP
100 g/3¼ oz sugar
125 ml/4 fl oz water
250 ml/8 fl oz honey

Sprinkle the yeast over the water and let stand until dissolved, stirring once, for about 5 minutes. Sift the flour and salt into a large bowl, and make a well in the centre. Add the milk, eggs and dissolved yeast to the well. Stir with a wooden spoon, gradually drawing in flour to make a thick sticky batter. The batter should fall from the spoon, so add more water to soften it if necessary. Beat the batter until the texture is smooth and elastic, 3-4 minutes. Cover with a damp cloth and leave to rise in a warm place until doubled in bulk, 1½ -2 hours.

Make the honey syrup: combine the sugar, water and honey in a saucepan and heat gently, stirring occasionally, until bubbly and the sugar is dissolved. Bring to the boil and simmer until syrupy, 12-15 minutes. Keep warm while frying the fritters.

Heat the oil for deep-frying to 180°C/360°F – a bit of batter dropped in it will sizzle briskly. Beat the batter with the spoon to knock out air. Using two teaspoons, drop spoonfuls of batter into the hot oil and fry until done, 3-4 minutes. Drain on paper towels and keep warm in a low oven while frying the remaining fritters.

Transfer the fritters to serving plates and sprinkle with cinnamon and nutmeg. Serve at once, passing warm honey syrup separately.

Peaches and ice cream with salty caramel sauce

It was a renowned Burgundian chef who first thought of adding salted butter to caramel sauce, giving it a subtle, piquant edge. Delicious hot or cold, you can keep this sauce on hand in the refrigerator. Pull it out at the last minute as a cold dip for grilled peaches, oranges or strawberries, or serve it hot with ice cream or pound cake.

SERVES 4

6 whole peaches
3 tablespoons dark brown sugar
3 tablespoons butter
vanilla ice cream (for serving)

FOR THE SALTY CARAMEL SAUCE
200 g/6½ oz sugar
250 ml/8 fl oz double cream
60 g/2 oz salted butter

Preheat the grill. Halve the peaches, discarding the stones, and set them cut sides up in a buttered baking dish. Sprinkle them with brown sugar and dot with the butter. Grill them about 7.5 cm/3 inches from the heat until the peaches are tender and starting to brown, 7-10 minutes.

Meanwhile, make a dark caramel syrup: in a heavy-based saucepan, heat the sugar and 125 ml/4 fl oz water, stirring only once or twice, until the sugar dissolves. Boil rapidly without stirring until the syrup begins to brown around the edge of the pan. Continue cooking over medium heat until done, 1-2 minutes, swirling the pan occasionally so the syrup colours evenly. Once it starts to brown, it will colour quickly.

When the caramel is dark, remove the pan from the heat and let the bubbles subside. Add the butter, stir until smooth and then pour in the cream. Stand well back, as the caramel will sputter and foam when butter and cream are added.

To serve: transfer hot peaches to individual plates and spoon over any juice. Add a scoop of vanilla ice cream. If necessary, reheat the sauce, stirring, until the caramel is completely dissolved and the sauce is hot. Spoon it over the peaches and serve at once.

Chocolate mousse with raspberries

Chocolate mousse can be cloyingly sweet, so I like to add a surprise layer of tart fresh raspberries. For best results, use the finest dark chocolate and leave the mousse to mellow for at least 6 hours before serving.

SERVES 4

250 g/8 oz raspberries

175 g/6 oz best dark chocolate, chopped

125 ml/4 fl oz water

3 eggs, separated

1 tablespoon raspberry liqueur or Cognac

3 tablespoons sugar

FOR THE CHANTILLY CREAM

125 ml/4 fl oz double cream

1 tablespoon sugar

2 teaspoons raspberry liqueur or Cognac

four 125-ml/4-fl-oz mousse pots or ramekins; pastry bag with medium star tube

Pick over the raspberries, rinsing only if they are sandy. Reserve 4 berries for decoration.

Heat the chocolate with 125 ml/4 fl oz water, stirring until melted. Simmer until slightly thickened, but still falling easily from the spoon, 1-2 minutes. Take from the heat and let for cool for 1-2 minutes. Beat the egg yolks into the chocolate, one by one, so they cook and thicken slightly. Beat in the liqueur or Cognac.

Stiffly beat the egg whites. Add the sugar and continue beating until the whites are glossy, about 30 seconds. Fold the egg whites into the warm chocolate mixture.

Pour half of the mousse mixture into the pots or ramekins. Spread the raspberries in a layer on top of the mousse and cover with the remaining mousse. Chill until set, at least 2 hours.

Shortly before serving, make the Chantilly cream: whip the cream until it holds soft peaks. Add the sugar and liqueur or Cognac and continue whipping until stiff enough to pipe. Transfer the cream to the pastry bag fitted with a star tube. Pipe one large rosette of cream on top of each mousse and top with a raspberry.

Serve chilled.

Pecan truffles

A chocolate truffle should be the ultimate rich mouthful, intense but not too sweet. Here, I've added a few chopped pecans to the ganache and then rolled the truffles in cocoa powder for a slightly bitter finish.

MAKES ABOUT 50 TRUFFLES

FOR THE GANACHE
45 g/1 ½ oz pecans
125 ml/4 fl oz double cream
175 g/6 oz best dark chocolate, finely chopped
1 tablespoon butter, softened

FOR THE COATING
250 g/½ pound plain chocolate, finely chopped
90 g/3 oz unsweetened cocoa powder, or more if needed

Preheat the oven to 175°C/350°F/gas4. Spread the nuts on a baking sheet, and toast in the preheated oven until lightly brown, 12-15 minutes, stirring once. Let cool slightly and then chop the nuts with a large knife or in a food processor, taking care not to overwork or they will become oily.

Make the ganache: bring the cream just to the boil and pour it over the dark chocolate in a bowl. Leave to melt for 2-3 minutes, then stir until smooth, if necessary warming for a few seconds over low heat. Chill without stirring until the ganache is cool but still soft, 8-12 minutes. Gently stir in the pecans and butter. Do not beat or the mixture will separate. Cover and chill until firm, 30-60 minutes.

Divide the ganache into 4 equal parts. Lightly dust a surface with cocoa powder and roll the ganache into 15-cm/6-inch logs about 1.25 cm/½ inch in diameter. Set the logs on a baking sheet lined with greaseproof paper. Chill until firm, 1-2 hours.

To coat and finish the truffles: melt the chocolate in a bowl over a pan of hot but not boiling water. Spread the cocoa in a shallow tray. Cut the logs into bite-size pieces. Dip the your palms in cocoa and roll the ganache pieces into balls. With two forks, dip these in the melted chocolate, drain off excess and roll in cocoa. Transfer to a tray lined with greaseproof paper and sprinkle with more cocoa. Chill until firm, 1-2 hours. Store in a cool place in an airtight container, layered with greaseproof paper.

Coconut ice cream

When making ice cream, for maximum taste I like to leave flavourings to infuse in the custard until the last possible moment. Here the grated coconut is strained out after the custard has thickened.

MAKES 1 LITRE/1 ⅔ PINTS

1 vanilla pod, split lengthwise, or ½ teaspoon vanilla essence
200 g/6½ oz sweetened shredded coconut
500 ml/16 fl oz milk
7 egg yolks
100 g/3¼ oz sugar
250 ml/8 fl oz double cream

ice-cream freezer

If using a vanilla pod, scrape the seeds from pod and add pod and seeds to the milk together with the coconut. Scald the milk, cover it and leave it over a low heat to infuse for 10-15 minutes.

Beat the egg yolks with the sugar until light and slightly thickened, 1-2 minutes. Whisk in half the hot milk, then stir this mixture back into the remaining milk. Heat the custard gently, stirring constantly with a wooden spoon, until it thickens slightly. Do not allow the custard to boil or it will curdle. Take from the heat at once and strain the custard into a bowl. Stir in the vanilla essence, if using. Cover tightly to prevent a skin forming and leave the custard to cool.

Pour the cool custard into the ice-cream freezer and churn until partially set. Whip the cream until it holds a soft peak. Add the whipped cream to the custard and continue churning until stiff. Transfer the ice cream to a chilled bowl, cover and store in the freezer. If making ahead, allow the ice cream to soften in the refrigerator for 1-2 hours before serving.

Camomile rose hip sorbet

Adjust the quantity of sugar in this sorbet according to its role, using less to cleanse the palate between courses and more for a soothing sweet dessert. You'll find the rose hips colour it an appealing pink.

MAKES 1 LITRE/1⅔ PINTS

10 camomile rose hip tea bags

FOR THE LEMON SYRUP

400 g/13 oz sugar, or more to taste

grated zest and juice of 2 lemons, or more if needed

ice-cream freezer

Make the lemon syrup: heat 500 ml/16 fl oz water with the sugar over low heat, stirring occasionally, until dissolved, then boil for 1-2 minutes. Stir in the lemon zest and juice and let cool.

Make the tea: bring 750 ml/1¼ pints water to the boil and add the tea bags. Remove from the heat and leave to infuse for 5-10 minutes before removing the bags.

Stir together the lemon syrup and the tea and leave to cool. Taste, adding more sugar or lemon juice if necessary. Pour into the ice-cream freezer and churn until stiff. Transfer to a chilled bowl, cover and store in the freezer.

If making ahead, allow the sorbet to soften in the refrigerator before serving for 30-60 minutes.

Apple rosemary jelly

Jelly needs an apple which is high in both pectin and in acid, and with that in mind I'd recommend you pick from the many interesting varieties now available. As I like a tart jelly, perfect with pork and duck, I add a minimum of sugar.

MAKES ABOUT 1 LITRE/1 $^2/_3$
  PINTS

1.8 kg/4 pounds apples
1 large bunch of rosemary
  (about 90 g/3 oz)
3 tablespoons black
  peppercorns
2 tablespoons cumin seeds
2 tablespoons coriander seeds
juice of 2 lemons
about 800 g/1$^3/_4$ pounds sugar

jelly bag (optional)
muslin

Scoop out the stem and flower ends of apples and quarter them, leaving the peel and cores. Put them in a large saucepan and cover with water (about 2 litres/3$^1/_3$ pints, there should be just enough almost to cover the fruit). Simmer, uncovered, stirring often, until fruit is very soft and falling apart, 1-1$^1/_4$ hours.

Prepare a jelly bag by dampening it and wringing it out. Alternatively, line a fine sieve with a clean damp cloth. Pour the apples into the jelly bag or sieve and let drip overnight into a large bowl. Note: squeezing the fruit clouds the jelly.

Meanwhile, prepare the herb and spices: coarsely chop the stalks and leaves of the rosemary. Put the peppercorns, cumin seed and coriander seeds in a thick plastic bag and crush with a rolling pin. Tie the rosemary and crushed spices securely in a piece of muslin.

Measure the apple juice and pour it into a large pan. Simmer the juice uncovered, skimming off any froth, 5 minutes. Meanwhile, measure 135 g/4$^1/_3$ oz sugar for each 250 ml/8 fl oz of apple juice. Add the sugar to the juice and heat gently, stirring occasionally, until the sugar dissolves. Add the lemon juice and the bag of herb and spices.

Bring to a rolling boil and cook to the setting point, 30-45 minutes, stirring often. Towards the end of cooking, skim off scum. Remove the herb bouquet, squeezing it against the side of the pot to extract all the flavours.

Let the jelly cool for 4-5 minutes, then ladle it into a heatproof measuring cup. Pour the jelly into sterilized jars and seal.

Old-fashioned raspberry jam

Ripe berries can be quite low in pectin, so to be sure this jam sets I always add a few unripe berries or a sliced tart apple.

MAKES ABOUT 1 LITRE/1 $\frac{2}{3}$
PINTS

1 kg/2 pounds ripe raspberries
600 g/1 $\frac{1}{4}$ pounds sugar
handful of unripe raspberries
**   or 1 tart apple**

Pick over the ripe and unripe raspberries, rinsing them only if they are sandy. Put alternating layers of the raspberries and sugar in a bowl. Cover and leave to macerate at room temperature for at least 8 hours or overnight.

Transfer the berries and sugar to a large pan. If using an apple, peel, core and thinly slice it and add to berries. Heat gently, stirring occasionally, until the sugar dissolves. Bring to a rolling boil and cook to the setting point, 20-30 minutes. Stir often and, towards the end of cooking, skim off scum.

Let the jam cool for 4-5 minutes, then ladle into a heatproof measuring cup. Pour the jam into sterilized jars and seal.

Breads, pancakes, cakes & pastries

Nothing is more typical of a nation's diet than the bread it makes from the local grain. The French repertoire of baguettes, pain de campagne and croissants depends on the medium gluten wheat flour found in France. In Portugal, cornmeal and olive oil are added to wheat flour for chewy broa. Scandinavia and central Europe are famous for rye breads and pumpernickel. Further south, in Morocco, the flour is soft, making light, delicate bread, often flavoured with aniseed or sesame. None of them are difficult to make or require rare ingredients.

In this chapter we also look at ethnic breads like pitta and naan, as well as at the amusing range of tea breads, crêpes and pancakes that can be mixed and

baked in minutes, thanks to baking powder and bicarbonate of soda.

As for cakes, I've started with basic sponge in the form of a traditional French *génoise*, then there's a run through several other classics, including incredibly frothy and light angel food cake, pound cake – the queen of the creamed cakes – Swiss roll, fruit cake in its festive form, batter breads, nutty tortes and moist rich cheesecakes. For pastries, there are pies and tartlets with all manner of fillings, crunchy heart-shaped palmiers, and feather-light meringues. There are even some chocolate cookies and a few savoury pastries, including a fennel and Roquefort quiche and Greek *spanakopitta* – spinach and feta cheese sandwiched in layers of filo pastry – and, of course, that most delightful of mouthfuls, the cheese choux puff.

Sourdough rye bread

The sourdough starter used for this robust and tasty bread is flavoured with whole onion.

MAKES 2 LARGE LOAVES

500 g/1 lb strong white flour

1 tablespoon salt

**300 g/10 oz rye flour, or more if
needed**

375 ml/12 fl oz lukewarm water

10 g/⅓ oz caraway seeds

**1 egg beaten with 1 tablespoon
water for glazing**

FOR THE STARTER

**1 tablespoon/10 g/⅓ oz dried
yeast**

500 ml/16 fl oz lukewarm water

300 g/10 oz rye flour

1 large onion, halved

First make the starter: sprinkle the yeast over half the water in a bowl and let stand until dissolved, stirring once, about 5 minutes. Stir in the rye flour with your hand to form a smooth dough, then stir in the remaining water to make a thick but pourable batter. Push the onion halves into the mixture until completely submerged. Cover with a damp cloth and leave to ferment in a warm place to allow flavour to develop for at least 24 hours and up to 3 days.

Sift the white flour with the salt into a large bowl. Stir in the rye flour and make a well in the centre. Discard the onion from the starter, stir to knock out air and add to the well with the water and the caraway seeds. Mix with your hand, gradually drawing in flour to make a smooth dough. The dough should be sticky and slightly wet. If necessary, work in more rye flour.

Brush a large bowl with vegetable oil. Turn the dough out on a work surface and knead until soft, smooth and slightly elastic, 8-10 minutes, sprinkling with rye flour if it sticks to the surface. Alternatively, the dough can be mixed and kneaded in a heavy-duty electric mixer. Put dough in the oiled bowl and flip so the surface is oiled. Cover with a damp cloth and let rise in a warm place until doubled in bulk, 1½-2 hours.

Sprinkle 2 baking sheets with rye flour. Turn the dough out on the work surface, knead lightly to knock out air and divide it in half. Pat each half into an oval and roll lengthwise into a tight cylinder, pinching the edge to seal as a seam. Gently roll each cylinder back and forth on a work surface to lengthen it. Place the loaves seam sides down on the prepared baking sheets. Cover the loaves with a floured cloth and let rise in a warm place until doubled in bulk, 45-60 minutes.

Preheat the oven to 190°C/375°F/gas5. Place a roasting pan on the oven floor or on the lowest rack. Brush the loaves with egg glaze and make 5 diagonal slashes, about 6 mm/¼ inch deep, in the top of each loaf. Put the loaves in the preheated oven and throw 2 handfuls of ice cubes into the heated roasting pan to make steam. Bake the loaves until done, 35-45 minutes. Remove them and transfer to a rack to cool.

Light wholemeal loaf

Many wholemeal loaves are dense and chewy, so I find this light but full-flavoured bread particularly useful. This large loaf is perfect for hearty sandwiches, but the dough can easily be baked in smaller pans for more manageable loaves. Use a full-bodied honey, as the flavour comes through clearly.

MAKES I LARGE LOAF

I tablespoon honey

425 ml/14 fl oz lukewarm water

10 g/⅓ oz dried yeast

**250 g/8 oz strong white flour,
or more if needed**

I tablespoon salt

**250 g/8 oz wholemeal flour, or
more if needed**

**23x13x7.5-cm/9x5x3-inch loaf
pan**

Stir the honey and water in a small bowl until mixed. Sprinkle the yeast over the honey mixture and let stand until dissolved, stirring once, about 5 minutes.

Sift the white flour and salt into a large bowl. Stir in half the wholemeal flour and make a well in centre. Pour the yeast mixture into the well. Mix with your hand, gradually drawing in the flour to make a smooth thick batter. Work in the remaining wholemeal flour a little at a time, adding enough to make a dough which pulls away from the sides of the bowl in a ball. It should be soft and slightly sticky.

Brush a large bowl with vegetable oil. Turn the dough out on a floured work surface and knead until it is smooth and elastic, 8-10 minutes, sprinkling with plain flour if it sticks to the surface. Alternatively, the dough can be mixed and kneaded in a heavy-duty electric mixer. Put the dough in the oiled bowl and flip so the surface is oiled. Cover with a damp cloth and let the dough rise in a warm place until doubled in bulk, 1-1½ hours.

Brush the loaf pan with oil. Turn the dough out on a work surface and knead lightly to knock out air. Pat the dough into an oval longer than the pan. Roll the oval into a tight cylinder, seam side up, and fold in the ends so the cylinder is the length of the pan. Place the dough seam side down in the prepared pan. Cover the loaf with a dry cloth and let rise in a warm place until risen to top of pan, 45-60 minutes.

Preheat the oven to 190°C/375°F/gas5. Sprinkle the top of the loaf with plain flour and brush away any excess. Bake in the preheated oven until done, 45-60 minutes. Transfer to a rack and let cool for 5 minutes. Turn the loaf out of the pan and leave on the rack to cool completely.

Skillet cornbread with herbs

For colour, I usually use yellow cornmeal for cornbread, but white cornmeal tastes equally good. For a sweeter cornbread, simply double the sugar in this recipe. For a rich and savoury cornbread, fry some bacon in the pan and use the drippings instead of butter to coat the pan. Pouring the batter into a hot pan makes for a crispy crust.

SERVES 6-8

125 g/4 oz plain flour

1 tablespoon baking powder

175 g/6 oz fine yellow or white cornmeal

1 tablespoon sugar

1½ teaspoons salt

2 eggs

60 ml/2 fl oz melted butter

300 ml/½ pint milk

2 tablespoons mixed chopped herbs such as rosemary, sage and thyme

25-cm/10-inch skillet or deep ovenproof frying pan

Preheat the oven to 220°C/425°F/gas7. Thoroughly butter the skillet or frying pan and heat it in the oven.

Sift the flour and baking powder into a large bowl. Stir in the cornmeal, sugar and salt and make a well in the centre. In another bowl, whisk the eggs, melted butter, milk and herbs until mixed and pour into the well. Stir together just until smooth.

Pour the batter into the hot skillet or frying pan and tap the pan on the work surface to smooth the top of the batter. Bake in the preheated oven until done, 20-25 minutes. Brush the bread with melted butter while hot to soften the crust. Serve at once.

Jewish egg bread *Challah*

This Jewish bread is ancient, baked to bring to temple on holidays and the Sabbath – *challah* **means 'offering.' The bread is usually, but not always, plaited.**

MAKES 1 LARGE LOAF

10 g/⅓ oz dried yeast

250 ml/8 fl oz lukewarm water

60 ml/2 fl oz vegetable oil

50 g/1¾ oz sugar

2 eggs, beaten until mixed

2 teaspoons salt

550 g/18 oz strong white flour, or more if needed

1 egg yolk mixed with 1 tablespoon water for glazing

1 teaspoon poppy seeds for sprinkling

Sprinkle the yeast over 3-4 tablespoons of the water and let stand until dissolved, stirring once, about 5 minutes. Add the oil and sugar to the remaining water and stir until the sugar dissolves.

In a large bowl, combine the eggs with the salt, dissolved yeast and the water, oil and sugar mixture. Stir in half the flour and mix well with your hand. Work in the remaining flour, a little at a time, adding enough to make a dough which pulls away from the sides of the bowl in a ball. It should be soft and slightly sticky.

Brush a large bowl with oil. Turn the dough out on a floured work surface. Knead the dough by picking it up and slapping it down on the work surface. Continue kneading the dough until it is smooth and very elastic, 5-8 minutes. Alternatively, the dough can be mixed or kneaded in a heavy-duty electric mixer. Put the dough in the oiled bowl and flip so the surface is oiled. Cover with a damp cloth and let the dough rise in a warm place until doubled in bulk, 1-1½ hours.

Brush a baking sheet with oil. Turn the dough out on the work surface and knead lightly to knock out air. Cut the dough into 3 equal pieces. Roll each piece under the palms of your hands to form a long strand, stretching and tapering each end. Line the strands up next to each other. Starting in the centre and working towards one end, braid the strands, stretching them as you move towards the end to accentuate the taper. Turn the dough and braid the other half. The loaf should be fattest in the centre. Pinch the ends and tuck them under the braid. Transfer the braided loaf to the baking sheet. Cover with a dry cloth and let rise in a warm place until doubled in bulk, 45-60 minutes.

Preheat the oven to 190°C/375°F/gas5. Brush the loaf with egg glaze and sprinkle with poppy seeds. Bake in the preheated oven until done, 35-40 minutes. Transfer the bread to a wire rack to cool.

Indian wholemeal flat bread *Naan*

Naan **is the basic bread of the Indian subcontinent, its ingredients varying only slightly from region to region. Though traditionally baked in a** *tandoor* **oven, the dough still puffs well in a standard oven set on the highest heat.** *Naan* **can be served hot or at room temperature.**

MAKES 6

1 teaspoon sugar

2 tablespoons warm water

7 g/¼ oz dried yeast

175 g/6 oz plain flour

1 teaspoon salt

175 g/6 oz wholemeal flour, or more if needed

175 ml/6 fl oz lukewarm milk

175 ml/6 fl oz plain yogurt

Combine the sugar and water and stir until the sugar dissolves. Sprinkle the yeast over the sugar mixture and let stand until dissolved, stirring once, about 5 minutes. Brush a bowl with vegetable oil.

Sift the plain flour and salt into a large bowl, stir in the wholemeal flour and make a well in the centre. Stir the milk and yogurt into the yeast mixture and pour into the well. Mix with your hand, gradually drawing in the flour, to make a soft dough. The dough should be wet and slightly sticky. If necessary, work in more wholemeal flour. Turn the dough out on a floured work surface and knead until it is smooth and elastic, 5-8 minutes. Alternatively, the dough can be mixed and kneaded in a heavy-duty electric mixer.

Put the dough in the oiled bowl and flip so the surface is oiled. Cover with a damp cloth and let the dough rise in a warm place until doubled in bulk, 2-3 hours.

Turn the dough out on a work surface and knead lightly to knock out air. Shape the dough into a cylinder with your hands and cut it into 6 equal pieces. Roll each piece into a ball, place on an oiled plate, cover with lightly oiled cling film and let rest for 10-15 minutes.

Preheat the oven to 260°C/500°F/gas 10 or its highest setting and place a baking sheet near the top of the oven. Roll and stretch each ball of dough into a teardrop shape about 25 cm/10 inches long and 13 cm/5 inches at its widest.

Set 2-3 shaped naan on the hot baking sheet and bake in the preheated oven until puffed, with brown spots, 5-8 minutes. Remove from the oven and stack, covered with a cloth so the bread steams and softens. Continue baking the remaining breads. Serve hot or at room temperature.

Buckwheat pancakes *Blini*

Traditional Russian blini are made only with buckwheat flour, but I find they're lighter with a mixture of buckwheat and plain flours. On the other hand, the time-honoured accompaniments of caviar or smoked salmon with lemon wedges, sour cream and possibly melted butter can't be bettered. Buckwheat contains no gluten, so blini batter takes a long time to rise, but the wait is amply repaid in richness of flavour.

MAKES 12

500 ml/16 fl oz milk, or
   more if needed
10 g/⅓ oz dried yeast
125 ml/4 fl oz lukewarm water
125 g/4 oz plain flour
200 g/6½ oz buckwheat flour
½ teaspoon salt
3 eggs, separated
45 g/1½ oz melted butter
45 ml/1½ fl oz sour cream

griddle, skillet or heavy frying
   pan

Scald the milk and let cool to lukewarm. Sprinkle the yeast over the lukewarm water and let stand until dissolved, stirring once, about 5 minutes. Sift the flours and salt into a bowl. Make a well in the centre and pour in the yeast mixture with half the milk. Mix with your hand, gradually drawing in flour to make a smooth batter. Beat well for 2 minutes, cover with a damp cloth and let rise in a warm place until the batter is light and full of bubbles, about 2 hours.

With your hand, beat the mixture to knock out air. Beat in the remaining milk, followed by the egg yolks, melted butter and sour cream. The batter should be the consistency of double cream, but if too thick stir in more milk. Stiffly beat the egg whites and fold them into the batter. Cover and leave to stand for about 30 minutes longer.

Preheat the griddle, skillet or frying pan and brush lightly with butter. Pour in batter to make a 15-cm/6-inch round. Cook for 2-3 minutes until the underside is lightly browned and the top is bubbling, then turn and cook until done. Pile the blini on top of each other and keep warm while cooking the rest. Serve at once, with accompaniments of choice.

Belgian apple crêpes *Crêpes aux pommes caramelisées*

There's a back-street restaurant in Brussels which serves huge pots of steamed mussels, followed by these tantalizing crêpes, each set with a ring of caramelized apple. Use firm apples which hold their shape, such as Golden Delicious.

MAKES 12 CRÊPES, TO SERVE 4-6

**3 medium apples
   (about 500 g/1 lb)
2-3 tablespoons sugar
1 tablespoon ground cinnamon
2 tablespoons butter
icing sugar for sprinkling**

18-cm/7-inch crêpe pan

FOR THE BATTER

**60 g/2 oz flour
2 teaspoons sugar
$\frac{1}{4}$ teaspoon salt
3 eggs
250 ml/8 fl oz milk
grated zest of 1 lemon
75 g/2$\frac{1}{2}$ oz melted butter**

Make the batter: sift the flour, sugar and salt into a bowl, and make a well in the centre. Add the eggs and half the milk to the well and whisk until mixed. Continue stirring, gradually drawing in flour to make a smooth batter. Stir in half the remaining milk, cover and let stand at room temperature for 15-30 minutes.

Peel and core the apples and cut each into 4 rings, discarding the thin end pieces. In a small shallow bowl, combine the sugar and cinnamon. Dip the apple rings in the sugar and cinnamon mixture. Heat half the butter in a large frying pan. Add half the apple rings and fry briskly on both sides until caramelized. Transfer the rings to a plate and caramelize the remaining rings in the same way.

Fry the crêpes: stir the lemon zest and 2 tablespoons of the melted butter into the batter. The batter should be the consistency of thin cream; if thicker, stir in the remaining milk. Heat 2-3 teaspoons more butter in the crêpe pan until very hot. Add 2-3 tablespoons batter, turning and rotating the pan so the base is covered. At once, set an apple ring in the centre of the crêpe and drizzle over a little batter to cover it.

Fry the crêpe until browned, 1-2 minutes. Toss the crêpe, or turn with a palette knife and brown the other side. Transfer to a serving plate and keep warm. Continue frying the crêpes, overlapping 2-3 per plate per person. Sprinkle the crêpes lightly with icing sugar and serve at once.

Cranberry orange bread

In summer, when fresh cranberries are out of season, I use blueberries or gooseberries.

MAKES 1 MEDIUM LOAF

250 g/8 oz flour

150 g/5 oz sugar

¾ teaspoon baking powder

½ teaspoon salt

2 eggs

175 ml/6 fl oz milk

150 ml/5 fl oz vegetable oil

125 g/4 oz cranberries

grated zest of 1 orange

20x10x5-cm/8x4x2-inch loaf pan

Preheat the oven to 175°C/350°F/gas4. Butter the loaf pan and sprinkle with flour, discarding any excess.

Sift the flour, sugar, baking powder and salt into a large bowl and make a well in the centre. In a small bowl, whisk together the eggs, milk and oil. Add the egg mixture to the well and stir with a whisk until just mixed. Don't beat the batter or the bread will be heavy. Stir in the cranberries and orange zest.

Spoon the mixture into the pan, filling it two-thirds full. Bake on the lower rack of the oven until done, 1-1¼ hours. Let cool slightly, then turn out on a rack to cool. Serve warm or at room temperature.

SUMMER STRAWBERRY MINT MUFFINS

Preheat the oven to 200°C/400°F/gas6. Butter and flour 12 medium muffin cups. Prepare the batter as for the bread above, substituting hulled and chopped strawberries for the cranberries and 3 tablespoons chopped fresh mint for the orange zest. Pour into the cups and bake until done, 20-25 minutes.

Lemon génoise with lemon icing

The classic pan for génoise is a moule à manqué, with sloping sides. Unlike cakes baked in straight-sided pans, this cake is turned bottom up, so the warm icing runs evenly down the sloping sides. Lemon is my favourite flavouring, but orange or lime zest and juice can be used as well.

SERVES 6-8

60 g/2 oz butter
125 g/4 oz flour
pinch of salt
4 eggs
125 g/4 oz granulated sugar
grated zest of 1 lemon

FOR THE LEMON ICING
pared zest and juice of 1 lemon
200 g/6½ oz icing sugar, or
more if needed

23-cm/9-inch moule à manqué
cake pan

Preheat the oven to 175°C/350°F/gas4. Butter the base and sides of the cake pan, line the base with greaseproof paper and butter that. Sprinkle the pan with flour, discarding any excess. Warm the butter in a bowl over hot water until soft enough to pour, but do not allow it to melt to oil. Leave it to cool. Sift the flour with the salt.

Put the eggs, sugar and grated lemon zest in the bowl of a heavy-duty electric mixer and whisk until mixed. Turn the speed to high and continue whisking until the mixture is light and thick enough to leave a ribbon trail when the whisk is lifted, 8-10 minutes. If whisking by hand, set the bowl over a pan of hot but not boiling water, whisk the mixture to the ribbon stage, then take the bowl from the heat and whisk until cool.

Sift the flour over the egg mixture in 3 batches, folding in each as lightly as possible. Stir a little batter into the softened butter, then fold this mixture into the remaining batter. The batter will quickly lose volume after the butter is added. Pour the batter into the prepared pan and bake in the preheated oven until done, 35-40 minutes. When the cake is done, run a knife around the sides to loosen it and turn out on a rack. Leave it to cool.

To make the icing: cut the pared lemon zest into very fine julienne strips. Put these in a small pan of cold water, bring to the boil, simmer for 1 minute and drain. Sift the icing sugar into a small bowl. Stir in the lemon juice to make a stiff paste. Set the bowl in a bath of hot water and stir the icing until quite warm to the touch. It should lightly coat the back of a spoon. If too thick, thin it with a little water; if too thin, stir in more sifted icing sugar. Stir in the lemon zest and keep warm.

Pour the warm icing over the cake on the rack and spread with a palette knife so it flows down the sloping sides. Work quickly, as the icing will cool and set rapidly. Transfer the cake to a platter to serve.

Chocolate roll with espresso buttercream

I pipe buttercream rosettes along this roll and top them with chocolate coffee beans.

SERVES 8-10

45 g/1 $\frac{1}{2}$ oz flour

30 g/1 oz cocoa powder

$\frac{1}{2}$ teaspoon salt

4 eggs

125 g/4 oz granulated sugar

$\frac{1}{2}$ teaspoon vanilla essence

icing sugar for sprinkling

FOR THE ESPRESSO
  BUTTERCREAM FILLING

4 egg yolks

100 g/3 $\frac{1}{4}$ oz granulated sugar

250 g/8 oz best-quality unsalted butter

4 teaspoons instant espresso coffee dissolved in 2 tablespoons hot water, or more coffee to taste

FOR THE SUGAR SYRUP

60 g/2 oz granulated sugar

2 tablespoons Cognac (optional)

Preheat the oven to 190°C/375°F/5. Butter a 25x40-cm/10x16-inch baking sheet, line it with greaseproof paper and butter that. Sift together the flour, cocoa and salt.

Put the eggs, sugar and vanilla in the bowl of a heavy-duty electric mixer and whisk until mixed. Turn the speed to high and continue whisking until the mixture is light and thick enough to leave a ribbon trail when the whisk is lifted, 8-10 minutes. If whisking by hand, set the bowl over a pan of hot but not boiling water, whisk the mixture to the ribbon stage, then take the bowl from the heat and whisk until cool. Sift the flour over the egg mixture in three batches, folding in each as lightly as possible. Spread the batter evenly in a rectangle on the prepared baking sheet just to the edges of the sheet. Bake in the preheated oven until done, 8-10 minutes.

Slide the cake off the baking sheet on to a rack by gently pulling the paper with the cake on top. Turn the cake over on to a tea towel. Peel off the paper and roll the warm cake inside the towel, starting with a long side. Leave the rolled cake to cool.

Make the filling: beat the egg yolks in a large bowl until mixed. Heat the sugar with 5 tablespoons water until dissolved, bring to the boil and boil without stirring until the syrup reaches soft-ball stage (115°C/239°F). Gradually pour the hot syrup into the eggs, beating constantly, and continue to beat until the mix is cool and thick, about 5 minutes. Cream the butter and gradually beat it into the cooled egg mix (if warm, it will melt the butter). Beat in the coffee. Cover and chill until just firm, 15-30 minutes.

Meanwhile, make the sugar syrup: gently heat the sugar with 3 tablespoons of water, stirring occasionally until the sugar is dissolved. Boil until clear, about 1 minute. Remove from the heat and add the Cognac if you like.

Assemble the roll: unroll the cooled cake and trim the edges. Brush the cake with sugar syrup. Spread buttercream on the cake and roll up. Chill until firm, 1-2 hours.

Just before serving, sprinkle with icing sugar and trim the ends at an angle.

Angel food cake

There is some debate about the origins of this American confection, originally baked in a square tube pan. By the 1870s it was popular in Pennsylvania and New Jersey, a favourite among the thrifty Pennsylvania Dutch who still bake these cakes in order to use the egg whites left over from their traditional yolk-enriched noodles.

SERVES 10-12

300 g/10 oz sugar

125 g/4 oz soft cake flour

10-11 egg whites, at room temperature

1 teaspoon cream of tartar

1 teaspoon vanilla essence

½ teaspoon salt

25-cm/10-inch tube pan

Preheat the oven to 175°C/350°F/gas4 and set an oven rack in the bottom third of the oven. Note: do not grease the tube pan. Sift the sugar twice and set it aside. Sift together the flour and one-third of the sugar four times and set aside. Measure 375 ml/12 fl oz of egg white.

Beat the egg whites with a heavy-duty electric mixture on medium speed just until foamy, 1-2 minutes. Add the cream of tartar, 2 tablespoons cold water, the vanilla essence and salt. Continue beating, increasing the speed to medium-high, until the egg whites are very stiff but not dry, 4-5 minutes. Beat in the remaining sugar, 2 tablespoons at a time, until the egg whites are glossy and form a long peak when the whisk is lifted. Fold in the sifted flour and sugar mixture, 2 heaped tablespoonfuls at a time.

Spoon the batter into the ungreased tube pan and bake in the preheated oven until a skewer inserted in centre comes out clean, 40-45 minutes. Invert the cake while still in the pan, resting the pan on a funnel, thin-necked bottle or tea cups to keep it above the work surface. Leave the cake until set and thoroughly cool, about 1 hour. Run a knife around the edge of cake and ease it away from the sides of the pan. Invert on a rack and remove the pan.

To serve, cut the cake into wedges with a serrated knife or divide it into wedges with a special comb.

Hazelnut pound cake *Nusskuchen*

Toasted hazelnuts give this classic pound cake a rich flavour and crisp golden crust. For a warming winter combination, serve it with a chocolate sauce. In summer try vanilla ice cream.

SERVES 10-12

125 g/4 oz chopped hazelnuts
375 g/12 oz flour
1½ tablespoons baking powder
1 teaspoon salt
375 g/12 oz butter, softened
375 g/12 oz sugar
6 eggs
2 tablespoons instant coffee dissolved in 60 ml/2 fl oz milk
icing sugar, for sprinkling (optional)

25-cm/10-inch tube cake pan

Preheat the oven to 175°C/350°F/gas4. Spread the hazelnuts on a baking sheet and toast in the preheated oven until lightly brown, stirring once, 12-15 minutes. Let cool slightly, then grind the nuts in a food processor or using a rotary cheese grater. Do not overwork them or they will be oily.

Brush the cake pan generously with butter and sprinkle with flour, discarding the excess. Sift the flour with the baking powder and salt.

Cream the butter with an electric mixer or wooden spoon. Gradually beat in the sugar and continue beating until the mixture is light and fluffy, 4-5 minutes.

Beat the eggs into the butter mixture one by one, beating thoroughly between additions. If the mixture starts to separate, beat in a tablespoon of flour. Stir in the ground hazelnuts and dissolved coffee. Finally, sift the flour over the batter in three batches, folding in each batch as lightly as possible.

Spoon the batter into the prepared cake pan and bake in the preheated oven until done, 50-60 minutes. Let cool for 5 minutes, then turn out on a wire rack to cool completely. Just before serving, sprinkle the cake with icing sugar.

Mrs Green's Christmas cake

This recipe takes us back 100 years to Victorian England and Mrs Green, who was a cook in a great house with more than a dozen in the family. She would double or triple this recipe, using her hands to warm and dissolve the sugar, making mixing easy.

SERVES 12-16

375 g/³⁄₄ lb flour

¹⁄₂ teaspoon freshly grated nutmeg

¹⁄₂ teaspoon ground allspice

¹⁄₂ teaspoon salt

125 g/4 oz candied cherries

125 g/4 oz chopped candied orange peel

375 g/³⁄₄ lb butter, softened

375 g/³⁄₄ lb sugar

6 eggs, at room temperature

500 g/1 lb seedless raisins

125 g/4 oz flaked almonds

3 tablespoons Cognac

25-cm/10-inch springform pan

Preheat the oven to 150°C/300°F/gas2. Generously brush the springform pan with butter, line the base and sides with greaseproof paper and butter the paper. Sprinkle the pan with flour, discarding excess.

Sift the flour with the nutmeg, allspice and salt. Put the cherries in a small pan of cold water, bring to the boil and boil for 30 seconds to rinse away any syrup or sugar. Drain the cherries on paper towels and coarsely chop them. In a small bowl, toss the cherries and candied orange peel in 2-3 tablespoons of the flour.

With your hand or using an electric mixer, cream the butter in a large bowl. Beat in the sugar until the mixture is soft and light, 8-10 minutes. Beat in the eggs one at a time, beating well between additions – if the mixture starts to separate, beat in a little flour between each egg. With your hand or a wooden spoon, stir in remaining flour in three batches. Finally, mix in the cherries, orange peel, raisins, flaked almonds and Cognac.

Transfer the batter to the prepared pan, leaving a shallow depression in the centre. Bake the cake in the preheated oven until done, 2-3 hours.

Leave the cake to cool in the pan. When cooled completely, unmould the cake and wrap it in muslin. Store in an airtight container for at least a month and up to a year, basting from time to time with rum, brandy or port.

Chef Chambrette's almond torte

After 50 years in the restaurant business, Chef Chambrette is a master at making the most of what he has. From just three basic ingredients – almonds, egg whites and sugar – he makes this crunchy golden torte. If you like, decorate it with a trail of melted dark or white chocolate.

SERVES 6-8

90 g/3 oz sliced almonds
250 g/8 oz ground almonds
125 g/4 oz icing sugar, sifted
whites of 4 eggs
2 tablespoons granulated sugar
$\frac{1}{2}$ teaspoon vanilla essence
grated zest of 2 lemons
pinch of salt

23-cm/9-inch springform pan

Preheat the oven to 160°C/325°F/gas3. Butter the base and sides of the cake pan, line the base with greaseproof paper and butter that. Sprinkle the base and sides of the pan with sliced almonds and chill until set, at least 15 minutes. Mix the ground almonds with icing sugar.

Meanwhile, make the batter: stiffly beat the egg whites, using a heavy-duty electric mixer or by hand, ideally in a copper bowl. Add the granulated sugar and continue beating until the egg whites are glossy and form a long peak when the whisk is lifted, about 1 minute more. Stir in the vanilla, lemon zest and salt. Fold in the ground almond and icing sugar mixture in three batches.

Pour the batter into the prepared pan and tap on the counter to expel air bubbles. Bake until done, 40-45 minutes.

Remove the torte and let it cool completely before unmoulding.

Classic American cheesecake

**Snowy white and inches high, rich creamy cheesecake is an American dream. There are
endless variations and all kinds of tricks, but the real secret is to use ordinary
packaged cream cheese with nothing fancy added. Prepare at least a day ahead, to
allow it to chill. If you like, serve with a berry fruit coulis, to cut the richness.**

SERVES 12-16

**1 kg/2 lb cream cheese, at
  room temperature**
200 g/6½ oz sugar
1 teaspoon vanilla essence
½ teaspoon salt
4 eggs
finely grated zest of 1 lemon

Preheat the oven to 150°C/300°F/gas2. Brush the cake pan generously with butter.
Make the crust: melt the butter, stir in the biscuit crumbs and sugar. Press the
mixture into the bottom of the pan, spreading it evenly with the back of a spoon.
Bake until lightly toasted, 13-15 minutes. Remove and leave to cool on a rack.

Make the cheesecake: in a heavy-duty electric mixer on low speed, beat the cream
cheese until soft. Use the paddle attachment instead of the whisk, so air is not

FOR THE CRUST
75 g/2 ½ oz butter
200 g/6 ½ oz dry biscuit
  crumbs, such as gingersnap
  or cream cracker
45 g/1 ½ oz sugar

23-cm/9-inch springform pan

beaten into the mixture. Add the sugar, vanilla and salt, and continue beating until light and creamy, 3-4 minutes. Add the eggs, one by one, beating until smooth. Stir in the lemon zest. Pour the batter into the cake pan and bake in the preheated oven until done, 1-1 ½ hours.

Turn the oven off, open the door slightly and leave the cake to cool for 1 hour. Transfer to the refrigerator and chill for at least 12 hours or overnight.

To serve, warm the sides of the pan with your hands to melt the butter coating. Remove the ring from cake, loosening gently, if possible without using a knife. Set the cheesecake, with the pan base, on a plate.

Lemon meringues

The very first meringues are attributed to François Pierre de la Varenne, the founder of French classical cooking and after whom I named La Varenne Cooking School.

MAKES ABOUT 20 MERINGUES
200 g/6 ½ oz sugar
grated zest of 1 lemon
whites of 4 eggs

Preheat oven to 110°C/225°F/gas ¼ and line a baking sheet with non-stick baking paper.

Stiffly beat the egg whites. Add 3 tablespoons of the sugar and continue beating until the whites are glossy, 1-2 minutes. Add the remaining sugar and beat 1-2 minutes until the meringue is perfectly beaten. Stir in the lemon zest.

Using 2 teaspoons, drop rounded spoonfuls of mixture on the baking sheet, leaving room for them to spread slightly. Bake until done, 1-1 ½ hours. Transfer them to a rack and let them cool completely. They will crisp as they cool.

Pear and almond cream tartlets *Tartelettes aux poires normande*

Look for pears just shorter than the diameter of your moulds, or trim to fit before slicing.

MAKES 8

4 ripe pears
sugar for sprinkling
3-4 tablespoons apricot jelly

FOR THE FRENCH SWEET PIE
PASTRY
275 g/9 oz flour
$\frac{1}{2}$ teaspoon salt
125 g/4 oz sugar
4 egg yolks
I teaspoon vanilla essence
125 g/4 oz butter

FOR THE ALMOND CREAM
100 g/3 $\frac{1}{4}$ oz butter, softened
100 g/3 $\frac{1}{4}$ oz sugar
I egg and I egg yolk, lightly
beaten
100 g/3 $\frac{1}{4}$ oz ground almonds
pinch of salt

eight 10-cm/4-inch tartlet
moulds
6-inch/15-cm round pastry
cutter (optional)

Make the pastry: sift the flour on to a work surface and make a well in the centre. Combine the salt, sugar, egg yolks and vanilla in the well and mix with your fingers. Pound the butter with a rolling pin to soften slightly, add to the well and quickly work in to the other ingredients. Gradually draw in flour from the sides and continue working with the fingers of both hands until coarse crumbs form. Press the pastry into a ball.

Knead the pastry with the heel of your hand, pushing it away and gathering it up until it is smooth, pliable and pulls away from the work surface in one piece, 1-2 minutes. Shape into a ball, wrap it and chill until firm, at least 30 minutes.

Meanwhile, make the almond cream: beat the butter with an mixer or wooden spoon until creamy. Gradually beat in the sugar and continue beating vigorously until light and soft. Gradually add the eggs, beating well after each. Fold in the almonds and salt.

Preheat the oven to 200°C/400°F/gas6. Put a baking sheet in the lower third of the oven to heat. Brush the tartlet moulds with butter. Roll out the pastry to a thickness of 6 mm/$\frac{1}{4}$ inch. Cut 8 rounds of pastry with the biscuit cutter or using a 15-cm/6-inch pan lid as a guide, rerolling the pastry if necessary. Line the tartlet moulds with the rounds, pressing them well into the bottoms and evenly up the sides to form neat cases. Chill until firm, about 15 minutes.

Meanwhile, peel the pears, halve them lengthwise and scoop out the cores. Cut the pear halves across in 6-mm/$\frac{1}{4}$-inch slices and flatten the slices slightly. Spoon the almond cream into the tartlet cases, spreading it evenly. Using a palette knife, lay a pear half on top of the cream in each case. Sprinkle with a little sugar.

Bake the tartlets on the baking sheet until pastry and almond cream are a rich golden brown, 15-20 minutes. Let cool slightly before unmoulding. Shortly before serving, make the apricot glaze: heat the apricot jelly and 2 tablespoons water in a small pan, stirring until melted. Brush tartlets with the glaze and serve at room temperature.

Giant palm leaves *Palmiers*

For savoury palm leaves, use grated Parmesan cheese instead of the sugar.

MAKES ABOUT 28
**400 g/13 oz sugar, more if
    needed**

FOR THE PUFF PASTRY
500 g/1 lb flour
2 teaspoons salt
500 g/1 lb butter, softened
**250 ml/8 fl oz ice water, more if
    needed**

For the basic pastry: sift flour and salt on a surface and make a well in the centre. Add 30-45 g/1-1½ oz butter, cut into pieces, to the well with the water. Work with your fingers until well mixed, then gradually draw in flour to make crumbs. Work just until the pastry is mixed, adding more water if dry. Shape into a ball, cover and rest in the refrigerator for 15 minutes. Don't overwork pastry, it should be quite rough.

Lightly flour remaining butter, put between sheets of greaseproof paper and flatten with a rolling pin. Fold, wrap and continue pounding and folding until pliable but not sticky – the consistency of the pastry. Shape butter into a 15-cm/6-inch square and flour lightly. Roll pastry to a 30-cm/12-inch square, slightly thicker in the centre. Set butter diagonally in the centre, and fold pastry around it like an envelope. Pinch edges to seal. Flatten pastry package slightly with rolling pin and turn over. Roll to a 45x15-cm/18x6-inch rectangle. Fold over one of the short sides, then the other, so rectangle is folded in three layers, like a letter, and forms a square. Press open ends lightly with the pin to seal. Turn 90 degrees to bring open edges towards you. Roll again and fold in three. Wrap and rest in the refrigerator, until firm, 20-30 minutes. Give it two more turns and rest again for 20-30 minutes. Give the pastry two more turns, wrap and chill for 30 minutes.

Roll again to a 50x20-cm/20x8-inch rectangle on a surface sprinkled generously with sugar. Sprinkle with more sugar, fold in three to a square, turn and roll again. Sprinkle with sugar, fold and chill for 30 minutes. Roll about 6 mm/¼ inch thick to a 55x36-cm/23x14-inch rectangle. Trim sides and sprinkle with sugar. Fold each short side to meet in the centre. Sprinkle with sugar and fold short sides to centre again. Bring one folded side on top of the other and press down lightly. Chill until firm, 15-30 minutes.

Cut into 1.25-cm/½-inch slices (they'll be heart-shaped). Set on a water-sprinkled baking sheet. Open slices slightly so they are looser, with a curve at the top of the heart to encourage rising. Chill for 15 minutes. Preheat oven to 220°C/425°F/gas7. Bake, turning once or twice so they brown and caramelize thoroughly, 15-20 minutes.

Chocolate chunk macadamia cookies

Nothing tastes quite like these rich biscuits studded with chunks of dark chocolate and chopped macadamia nuts. Our adult children still wolf them down with a tall glass of milk.

MAKES 16 LARGE BISCUITS

175 g/6 oz dark chocolate
100 g/3¼ oz macadamia nuts
225 g/7¼ oz flour
½ teaspoon bicarbonate of soda
pinch of salt
90 g/3 oz butter, softened
50 g/1¾ oz brown sugar
100 g/3¼ oz granulated sugar
1 egg
½ teaspoon vanilla essence

Preheat the oven to 190°C/375°F/gas5. Brush a baking sheet with butter. With a large knife, chop the chocolate into rough chunks. Coarsely chop the macadamia nuts. Sift together the flour, bicarbonate of soda and salt.

In a large bowl, beat the butter until soft. Gradually add the mixed sugars and continue beating until light and fluffy. Beat in the egg and vanilla. Add the flour mixture in two batches, stirring just until mixed. Stir in the chocolate chunks and chopped nuts.

Drop tablespoonfuls of the batter on the prepared baking sheet, leaving room in between each, as the biscuits will spread during baking.

In batches if necessary, bake in the preheated oven until done and nicely coloured around the edges, 12-15 minutes.

Let the biscuits cool slightly, then transfer them to a wire rack to allow them to cool completely.

Fennel and Roquefort quiche

Sharp Roquefort works well with this aromatic fennel custard filling, but other firm blue cheeses are fine.

SERVES 6-8

750 g/1 ½ lb fennel bulbs, trimmed and sliced

30 g/1 oz butter

2 tablespoons chopped thyme

salt and pepper

175 g/6 oz Roquefort cheese, crumbled

FOR THE FRENCH PIE PASTRY

200 g/6½ oz flour

100 g/3¼ oz butter, softened

1 egg yolk

½ teaspoon salt

45 ml/1½ fl oz water, or more if needed

FOR THE CUSTARD

1 egg, plus 1 extra egg yolk

125 ml/4 fl oz milk

60 ml/2 fl oz double cream

pinch of grated nutmeg

25-cm/10-inch tart pan with removable base

Make the French pie pastry: sift the flour on to a work surface and make a well in the centre. Pound the butter with a rolling pin to soften it. Put the butter, egg yolk, salt and water into the well. With the fingers, work the moist ingredients until thoroughly mixed. Draw in the flour and work in the other ingredients with the fingers of both hands until coarse crumbs form. If the crumbs are very dry, add 1-2 tablespoons more water. Press the pastry into a ball. Lightly flour a work surface. Blend the pastry by pushing it away from you with the heel of your hand, then gathering it up until it is very smooth and peels away from work surface in one piece, 1-2 minutes. Shape into a ball, wrap and chill.

Roll out the pastry, use to line the tart pan and chill until firm, about 15 minutes. Preheat the oven to 220°C/425°F/gas7 and a baking sheet. Prick the base of the chilled pasty case with a fork, line with baking paper, weight with baking beans and set on the preheated baking sheet in the oven. Cook for about 10 minutes to partially blind-bake the pastry case. Take out and reduce oven to 190°C/375°F/gas5.

Prepare the fennel: heat the butter in a frying pan and add the fennel, thyme, pepper and just a little salt, as the cheese will be salty. Press a piece of buttered foil on top, cover and sweat, stirring occasionally, until very soft but not brown, 20-30 minutes.

Meanwhile, make the custard: in a bowl, whisk the egg, egg yolk, milk, cream, nutmeg, salt and pepper just until mixed.

When the fennel is soft, add the Roquefort cheese and stir to melt the cheese. Spread the mixture evenly in the base of the pastry case and pour over the custard. Gently mix the fennel mixture and custard with a fork.

Bake until done, 30-35 minutes. Let cool slightly before unmoulding. Serve warm or at room temperature.

Cheese choux puffs *Gougères*

For parties, make little ones the size of an apricot, but I love them big. Serve warm, still slightly soft in the centre.

MAKES 9 LARGE GOUGÈRES

100 g/3¼ oz flour

75 g/2½ oz butter

½ teaspoon salt

3-4 eggs

100 g/3¼ oz Gruyère cheese, coarsely grated

1 egg, beaten to mix with ½ teaspoon salt, for glazing

pastry bag fitted with 1.25-cm/½ -inch plain tube

Preheat the oven to 190°C/375°F/gas5. Line a baking sheet with baking paper. For the choux pastry: sift the flour on to a piece of baking paper. In a saucepan, heat 175 ml/6 fl oz water with the butter and the salt until butter melts, then bring to the boil. Immediately take from the heat, add the flour and beat vigorously with a wooden spoon until the mixture is smooth and pulls away from the sides of the pan to form a ball, 30-60 seconds. Beat over low heat to dry the mixture, 30-60 seconds.

Whisk 1 of the eggs in a bowl until mixed and set aside. With a wooden spoon or using an electric mixer, beat the remaining eggs into the dough one by one, beating thoroughly after each addition. Beat enough of the reserved egg into the dough so it is shiny and just falls from the spoon (not all the reserved egg may be needed). Beat in the cheese, reserving 2-3 tablespoons for sprinkling.

Put the dough in the pastry bag fitted with the plain tube and pipe nine 7-cm/2½ -inch mounds on the prepared baking sheet. Brush with egg glaze and sprinkle with the reserved cheese. Bake until done, 35-40 minutes. Let them cool slightly, then transfer to a rack.

Greek spinach and cheese pie *Spanakopita*

You'll often see filo pastry baked in individual parcels, but this large pie filled with spinach and feta cheese makes an eye-catching presentation.

SERVES 6-8

500 g/1 lb filo pastry

**60 g/2 oz butter, or more if
    needed**

**60 ml/2 fl oz olive oil, or more
    if needed**

FOR THE FILLING

1 kg/2 lb spinach

3 tablespoons olive oil

2 onions, finely chopped

pinch of freshly grated nutmeg

salt and pepper

**250 g/½ lb feta cheese,
    crumbled**

**small bunch of flat-leaved
    parsley, chopped**

**28-cm/11-inch tart pan with
    removable base**

Make the filling: tear the stems from the spinach leaves. Wash the leaves well in cold water and drain. Pack the spinach in a large heavy-based pan with just the water that clings, cover and cook just until wilted, stirring occasionally, 3-4 minutes. Let cool, then squeeze it to extract as much moisture as possible, then coarsely chop. Heat the olive oil in a large sauté pan. Add the onion and sauté, stirring, until soft but not brown, 3-4 minutes. Stir in the spinach, nutmeg and pepper. Cook, stirring, until very hot and any liquid has evaporated, about 2 minutes. Remove from the heat, stir in the cheese and chopped parsley. Adjust seasoning and let cool.

Preheat the oven to 175°C/350°F/gas4. Melt the butter with the olive oil. Brush the tart pan with some melted butter and oil. Lay a damp tea towel on the work surface. Unroll sheets of pastry on the towel. Using the tart pan as a guide, cut through all the sheets to make a round 7.5 cm/3 inches larger than the pan. Reserve trimmings for decoration. Cover sheets and trimmings with another damp towel.

Pull a filo round from under the damp towel and brush it lightly with melted butter and oil. Transfer to the tart pan, pushing it well into the bottom and sides. Repeat with half the sheets of filo, working quickly and brushing each layer with melted butter and oil. Keep the remaining sheets covered with damp towel.

Spoon the spinach and cheese mixture into the tart case, spreading it evenly. Top with the remaining filo sheets, brushing each layer, including the last, with oil and butter.

Fold the overhanging dough up around edge of tart pan, turning and pinching it to form a decorative edge. Cut the filo trimmings into 5-cm/2-inch wide strips. Crumple them lightly to make loose round flowers and arrange them on top of the pie so it is completely covered. Drizzle with the remaining melted butter and oil. Bake the pie in the preheated oven until done, 50-60 minutes. Let the pie cool slightly, remove from the tart pan and serve.